THRESHOLDS: RET
SPIRITUALITY THROU

Thresholds: Rethinking Spirituality Through Music

MARCEL COBUSSEN
Leiden University, The Netherlands

ASHGATE

Published by
Ashgate Publishing Limited
Gower House
Croft Road
Aldershot
Hampshire GU11 3HR
England

Ashgate Publishing Company
Suite 420
101 Cherry Street
Burlington, VT 05401-4405
USA

www.ashgate.com

British Library Cataloguing in Publication Data
Cobussen, Marcel, 1962–
   Thresholds : rethinking spirituality through music
   1. Spirituality in music 2. Music – Religious aspects 3. Music – Psychological aspects
   I. Title
   781.1'2

Library of Congress Cataloging-in-Publication Data
Cobussen, Marcel, 1962–
   Thresholds : rethinking spirituality through music / by Marcel Cobussen.
     p. cm.
   Includes bibliographical references and index.
   ISBN 978-0-7546-6479-6 (Hardback : alk. paper) – ISBN 978-0-7546-6482-6 (Paperback : alk. paper) 1. Spirituality in music. 2. Music – Religious aspects. 3. Music – Psychological aspects. I. Title.
   ML3921.C63 2008
   781'.12–dc22

                                         2007050739
ISBN   978-0-7546-6479-6 (Hbk)
         978-0-7546-6482-6 (Pbk)

Mixed Sources
Product group from well-managed forests and other controlled sources
www.fsc.org Cert no. SA-COC-1565
© 1996 Forest Stewardship Council

Printed and bound in Great Britain by
MPG Books Ltd, Bodmin, Cornwall.

Contents

List of Music Examples and Tables

Music Examples

Tables

Acknowledgements

As a scriptor, a composer of texts, I am first of all a reader and a listener. I wander around in other people's minds. I wander around in other people's books and essays, in other people's music. I bother friends and colleagues with my questions, with my doubts, with the problems I encounter while contemplating the project I am working on. Writing is selfish; at times unbearably, often unapproachably. The title of a book by the Spanish writer Jorge Semprun speaks volumes: *Writing or Living*. Writing takes place on a threshold. Parasitizing on other people's texts and unpublished thoughts, one carves out a space that is neither inside nor completely outside.

The sources of inspiration encountered during the realization of a book are endless. Several can be found in the bibliography as well as the index. Other sources seep into the material on a less traceable level; although their presence can be felt, their influence is not so concrete. And there are others who have contributed in yet another way; their mediation is not (only) discursive, but social and personal (as well). It is individuals and groups from this last category, whose help has been absolutely crucial for this project, who I would like to mention here.

Susan McClary and the whole Musicology Faculty at UCLA offered me generous hospitality as well as an inspiring intellectual environment during the fall semester of 2003. It was there that the first chapters of this book were produced. Lawrence Kramer's critical and erudite comments on large parts of the book motivated me to continue my quest as well as to re-adjust it. It was Geraldine Finn with whom I first discussed the relationship between music and spirituality. Her remarks on spirituality were instrumental in creating the very basis of this book. Through his direct commentary, good friend and colleague Ruud Welten helped me to find the right structure and appropriate music.

Steve Block was so kind as to share his (unpublished) analyses of John Coltrane's music with me. I gratefully used his work to found my arguments. Paul Scheepers and Barbara Bley have been sources of indispensable insight for the other musical analyses in this book.

Rokus de Groot and Sander van Maas from the Musicology Department of Amsterdam University and Niels Holger Petersen and his staff from the Theological Faculty at the University of Copenhagen offered me the opportunity to present and discuss more or less embryonic thoughts on the topic at issue.

The Netherlands Organization for Scientific Research, NWO, provided me in 2003 with a travel grant, making it possible for me to concentrate fully on this subject for almost half a year.

The Faculty of Creative and Performing Arts at Leiden University supported the materialization of this study in many different ways: besides the necessary institutional framework and administrative assistance, I was able to discuss relevant matters with my students in Leiden as well as Ghent.

Sharon Stewart turned this whole manuscript into idiomatic English. Additionally, she often inserted her own comments into the margins of my texts, which often lead to significant re-adjustments.

Traditionally, the last place is reserved for the one who has suffered the most: the partner. Ida, I hope it was worth the many hours we could have spent in another way.

Finally, I dedicate this book to my parents whose spiritual path I was not able to follow but whose education made it possible for me to rethink this subject at all.

THRESHOLD 1
The Desert in the Desert*

O<small>N</small> a dark desert highway, cool wind in my hair. Warm smell of colitas, rising up through the air. Up ahead in the distance, I saw a shimmering light. My head grew heavy, and my sight grew dim. I had to stop for the night. There she stood in the doorway; I heard the mission bell, and I was thinking to myself – this could be Heaven or this could be Hell. Then she lit up a candle, and she showed me the way. There were voices down the corridor; I thought I heard them say …[1]

You shake your head. Although a fresh breeze brushes against your face, its coolness is in vain. You are too tired. Your sight is no longer reliable; the eye/I is no longer in control. Everything becomes vague, unclear …

Everything? No, your ears are taking over. "The world is not for beholding. It is for hearing. It is not legible, but audible," Jacques Attali already declared in 1977 (Attali 1985: 3).

The ears easily identify the sounds coming from a distance: a mission bell and – though less clear – some mysterious human voices. The bell and the voices mark a threshold, the boundary between here and there, a 'there' that can be almost anything: another or an unknown world, heaven or hell … The music represents itself as and presents itself at the juncture between the here and the there, the threshold where one sheds the mastery of the eye/I. Sounds have their own distinctive relational qualities in the placing and spacing of experiences. Can 'Hotel California' be understood as the recognition of sound as a modality of knowing and being in the world? Can this song make us rethink the meaning, nature, and significance of certain experiences, of certain values and firmnesses? Does interaction with the sonic material of 'Hotel California' offer new possibilities to address issues of place, identity, belonging, memory? …

'Hotel California' announces … announces what actually? The practice of interpretation fails, precisely in its indefinite dissemination.[2] The song seems both

---

[*]   The title of this Threshold comes from Jacques Derrida's book *Acts of Religion* in which he states that the desert is an aporetic place, the most an-archic or an-archivable place: it is without a guaranteed entrance or way out, without a border region of which the map is predictable and the program is calculable. The 'desert in the desert' refers to a relation to the world, a relation to 'the other,' a spiritual relation perhaps, that is irreducible to knowledge, "there where one neither can nor should see coming what ought or could-*perhaps*-be yet to come. What is still left to come" (Derrida 2002: 47).

[1]   'Hotel California,' Words & Music by Don Henley, Glen Frey & Don Felder © 1976 Cass County Music, Red Cloud Music and Fingers Music. All rights administered by Warner/Chappell Music Ltd, London W6 8BS. Reproduced by permission.

[2]   On the web you can find many interpretations of 'Hotel California.' The Eagles themselves do not give a decisive answer as to what the lyrics mean. In an interview, guitar player and vocalist Glenn Frey says: "It is just all one shot, not necessarily, you know, just sort of strung together, and you sort of draw your own conclusions from it. So we are sort of trying to expand our lyrical horizons and just try to take out something in the bizarre."

to provoke and frustrate each interpretative pathway. It not only establishes itself within a difference in relation to all meaning; it produces its difference in making us believe that it contains hidden meaning. The lyrics lead one to suppose that one should understand something different from what one is given to hear ... A diabolical temptation ... To pretend to conceal is to seduce discourse, to give rise to it and simultaneously lead it astray. This is, however, precisely a way of positing *otherness*, the otherness of music, of outwitting interpretative colonizations, and of keeping, preserved from meaning, the pleasure of listening ...

"Last thing I remember, I was running for the door. I had to find the passage back to the place I was before ..."[3]

The secret of 'Hotel California,' the secret of all music perhaps, is to make you believe that it possesses some sayable secret. But writing can never be an entrance of meaning into music, an entry by way of the nameable; that door is blocked. The meaning of music lies in the keeping-at-a-distance of writing, reading, interpreting ...[4]

"You can check out any time you like, but you can never leave ..."[5]

[3]   'Hotel California,' Words & Music by Don Henley, Glen Frey & Don Felder © 1976 Cass County Music, Red Cloud Music and Fingers Music. All rights administered by Warner/Chappell Music Ltd, London W6 8BS. Reproduced by permission.

[4]   For this short meditation, I am greatly indebted to Michel de Certeau's book *The Mystic Fable*, especially pp. 50–5.

[5]   'Hotel California,' Words & Music by Don Henley, Glen Frey & Don Felder © 1976 Cass County Music, Red Cloud Music and Fingers Music. All rights administered by Warner/Chappell Music Ltd, London W6 8BS. Reproduced by permission.

THRESHOLD 2
A Short Prelude to
Music and Spirituality

You are on a threshold. The threshold of entering a book. And you have already crossed many before you arrived here; you have already dealt with many obstacles. It is impossible to say how many thresholds a book has: physical, psychological, economical, aesthetic, ethical, political, disciplinary, social, intellectual, cultural, temporal, and spatial ones (and all these on the levels of production, distribution, and reception) – the more you consider thresholds, the more of them you are aware of. Which is exactly one of the motivations for writing this book: to (re)think thresholds, to (re)think borders and limits, to (re)think the passage from one to the other, to pass through the passage, to stand still in and dwell upon the space between one and the other, between inside and outside, between here and there.[1] Because that is where a threshold can be located – located in a non-place, an *a*-topos, a space between, borderline and middle simultaneously.[2] A threshold – like a prelude – is a *para*-site: an undecided zone between inside and outside, neither here nor there, and, simultaneously, both here and there, both in and out. Inside and outside join and separate to form an undecidable play of perpetual displacement. The undecidability of the threshold's identity eradicates any thinking in clear oppositions, any binary ordering. A threshold joins by separating and separates by joining.[3] Furthermore, thinking thresholds means to abandon the idea that this 'third term' can ever be sublated by a dialectical method. The space between, the threshold, is the leaving of a remainder that cannot be thought within the framework of Western logocentrism, based on a dualistic logic; or, to state it more firmly, it is exactly what escapes this logocentric order. The book you are about to enter starts from the question: what does the preceding mean for our relation with music and spirituality.

---

[1] In *Statues* Michel Serres writes:

A door opens or closes a threshold which is held to be such because at this spot a law is overturned: on one side reigns a certain rule, on the other begins a new law, so that the door rests on its hinges on a neutral line where the two rules of law balance and cancel each other … The singular site is a part of neither this world nor the other or else it belongs to both. (Serres 1993: 90)

[2] "I prefer the middle," Hamm says to Clov in Beckett's *Endgame*.

[3] In his essay 'The Critic as Host,' J. Hillis Miller gives a very fine description of the activity of a para-site:

Para is a double antithetical prefix signifying at once proximity and distance, similarity and difference, interiority and exteriority, something inside a domestic economy and at the same time outside it, something simultaneously this side of a boundary line, threshold, or margin, and also beyond it, equivalent in status and also secondary or subsidiary, submissive, as of guest to host, slave to master. A thing in 'para,' moreover, is not only simultaneously on both sides of the boundary line between inside and out. It is also the boundary itself, the screen which is a permeable membrane connecting inside and outside. It confuses them with one another, allowing the outside in, making the inside out, dividing them and joining them. (Hillis Miller 1979: 219)

This is what I have done: writing (on) thresholds. Thresholds in a twofold sense: on the one hand, a threshold is part of a necessary opening leading from one place to another, a point of passage, a site of invitation, a mark of hospitality, such as when a groom carries his bride across the threshold of his house; on the other hand, the threshold is a stumbling block, a signal of discontinuity, a border, a checkpoint that not everybody can simply pass through without a certain effort. Admission and impediment – both are at work here; the one and the other, the one *in* the other, inseparable. Thresholds are ambivalent, because they constitute the medium in which opposites are opposed; they are the movement, the locus, and the play: (the production of) difference.

You are on the threshold of entering a book. Or are you already in? Did you already pass one or more thresholds? And are others already appearing? Known or unknown? Expected or unexpected? Easy or difficult thresholds?

Let us consider this book as a house, a hotel perhaps, a place with many rooms where you can roam endlessly, returning to earlier starting points, plotting new routes, but also pulling down certain walls and moving furniture from one room to another. Of course, you know that one does not necessarily gain access to a work of architecture by following the order of its production. You cannot even be sure that this house is built in the customary order, starting at its foundations and finishing at the roof ridge. Like so many others, this *Prelude* announces in the future tense ('this is what you are going to read') the conceptual content or significance of what will already have been written. In other words, from the viewpoint of this threshold (which is of course never the first one), which recreates an intention-to-say after the fact, the text exists as something written – a past – which, under the false appearance of a present, hidden, omnipotent author (in full mastery of his product), is presenting to you, the reader, as her or his future (Derrida 1981: 7). Time is always already out of joint when you enter a book. Like in music. Or in spirituality.

So, the book as a house, a hotel. With many rooms. And many occupants or temporary visitors. Many specters too: some hardly audible, others more prominently present even when they don't raise their voice. Rooms with different signatures, different functions, different atmospheres, different colors. And different sounds: every room in this book-house has its own music. One could say that each room has a different timbre in a twofold way. First, the conversations that are going on are held by different visitors. While some of the participants appear in more than one room, they will have other interlocutors so that their contributions will generate new resonances and reverberations. Second, the atmosphere in every room is determined to a great extent by the music which indicates and influences the direction the discourse will take. Still, it all takes place in one house, in this house, albeit an open house.

The topic that connects these various contributions: thresholds! So, I must already recant my earlier statement concerning rooms, because the house you are about to enter, that you have already – perhaps without noticing – entered, seems to consist only of thresholds, or – a word Borges uses – 'vestibules.' The thresholds are discussed on thresholds: there are only thresholds here, only borders, only a middle. Only beginnings too: everything begins on a threshold. The question posed in this house is if we are ever actually able to cross a threshold to enter a room with stable walls and dimensions. Perhaps we are always already condemned or invited to dwell on thresholds. Always on the way from the one to the other, from here to there, from now to later, that is, always detained, moving in a space between. Coming and going. Coming and going. Coming and going. Like music. Never there.

The threshold is an entrance, a beginning, which must not be confused with an origin. In one sense, every beginning has always already begun. In another sense, a beginning is unending.[4] With origins erased and conclusions never come to, we are left to roam, wander, and err along a margin that is ever the 'middest' (M. Taylor 1984: 98). So here we are: in the middle, that is, on the sill of a book that is supposed to be about music and spirituality, spirituality in music, spiritual music, musical spirituality. Rethinking spirituality through music, rethinking music through spirituality.[5] Which immediately raises the legitimate questions: what is meant by both music and spirituality, and, especially, by their mutual relation? What is this becoming spiritual of music and becoming musical of spirituality? How does one read these movements, this diagonally traversing of religious and artistic spaces? How do we recognize the spiritual in or through music? How is music able to invite the spiritual, how might it solicit the spiritual to appear?[6] Can spirituality in music be traced back to intrinsic musical qualities and characteristics? In other words, can spiritual music be reduced to one pole of some oppositional pairs: the spiritual *versus* the profane? Is the spiritual in music sweet, quiet, and peaceful, or, on the contrary, overwhelming and frightening? Reassuring and familiar, or challenging meaning, sense, and status quo by interrupting?[7]

Maybe these questions are not so much longing for clear answers as a stimulation towards an investigation of their workings, their appearances in certain (con)texts, their joint activity, their living together under the same roof, thereby already crossing some thresholds. In that sense, they will haunt (with) us.

What follows is the sketching of an outline of the relation between music and spirituality. This will be done by conducting ideas of spirituality through several musical sites. No rigid attempts are made to define spirituality before releasing it

---

[4]   "It is so difficult to find the beginning. Or better: it is difficult to begin at the beginning. And not try to go further back," Ludwig Wittgenstein writes in *On Certainty* (Wittgenstein, 1974: 62).

[5]   How do we still dare to use both 'music' and 'spirituality' singular?

[6]   The question I am raising here is how spirituality sounds. That is, I am not asking how the linguistically articulated concept 'spirituality' can be translated into music. The question is aiming at a spirituality that escapes language but which can be touched through music.

[7]   Georges Bataille, for example, demonstrates that the nature of the spiritual is not compatible with an unperturbed, almost self-evident entry to it; this is merely a humanized, safe spiritual, disposed of its dangerous and violent sides.

in these sites. Instead, the concept travels through them, firstly to constitute itself tentatively in the course of this trajectory and, secondly, to provisionally construe an interrelation between music and spirituality in the wake of its course. Thus, this relationship is something that comes to pass in an unfolding of thoughts that conveys itself as – is itself still (and always) – a work in progress.[8]

Directed by opening questions but not hindered by closing conclusions. "Ideas are never fixed but are always in transition; thus they are irrepressibly transitory," Mark C. Taylor writes (1984: 13). I hope this book is able to create a space for what might be labeled 'Nomad Thought' or 'ambulant science': unsettled and unsettling thought, slipping through the holes in the system within which it must, nevertheless, be registered.[9] Deterritorializing. Wandering in a space between, this book – less a complete than an open (perhaps broken) text – should also perform what it tries to speak about.[10]

Following Maurice Blanchot and Friedrich Hölderlin, for example, one could say that the spiritual is an open space, more specifically the space between the human and the divine world, the pure place where these two are separated. Thus, both writers do not define the spiritual as the absolute presence of the divine. Instead, they allocate a special and important role for the arts, poetry in particular: it should be the task of the arts to keep this space open, to keep it unoccupied. Thinking along with Blanchot and Hölderlin, I would like to present two further questions. Would it be possible that it is precisely art (music) that creates this open space, this space between? And would it be possible, perhaps even desirable and necessary, to redefine this space between the human and the divine world, thereby shifting the connotations from a putative transcendence to a more 'earthly' immanence?

Though only this threshold is adorned with the designation 'prelude,' it could be said that all following chapters are, in a way, preludes, prefaces, forewords, introductions, preliminaries, preambles, prologues, or prolegomena, if they are

---

[8]   Zen masters say that the questioning is already the way (*tao*). *Tao* already has a spiritual meaning, even before it is indicated which way is meant, and to where it may lead. An idea of the same kind can be found in the philosophy of Heidegger, defined as a thinking that calls or asks. Heidegger emphasizes the performing of this way of thinking, not its (possible) results.

[9]   I have found both the term 'Nomad Thought' and its exemplification in Mark Taylor's (1984) book *Erring*, though a major contribution is of course *Mille plateaux* by Gilles Deleuze and Félix Guattari. Nomad thought, minor or ambulant science, inhabits a 'more' that exceeds the space of reproduction (Deleuze and Guattari 1987: 374).

[10]   This reminds me of Schopenhauer when he writes that the striking of a chord or the dashes on a canvas carry away the imagination from all that is recognizable, sayable, familiar. However, just one word suffices to pull the imagination back; it knows again what it should hold on to. Understood this way, the word is the biggest enemy of art. Therefore, we should try to employ the word as if it is no longer a word, that is, by systematically evading every understandability and determination, and, through a strategy of ambiguity (Schopenhauer proposes the use of metaphors, metonyms, and allegories), create an untranslatable subject.

understood as points of departure, or rather as invitations to readers who might wish to turn these short, incomplete, and perhaps even impossible thought experiments into excursions of their own.[11] Perhaps impossible because these preludes never can or will be more than an outset or an opening, to use two other meanings of the word 'threshold.' They can never cross the border, transgress the limit, because they cannot speak the required *shibboleth*. The prelude as prelude is never part of the main text, of that of which it is the prelude. It always remains secondary to and in the service of that whose way it prepares. The suffix 'pre' immediately installs an exteriority. Within the current context, this means the recognition of a fundamental gap between what these preludes introduce and the subject bodies they are referring to: music and spirituality.[12] Neither of these two terms can be fully covered by discursivity. Language can never master them, never possess them. Which does not mean one should not speak, not write about them. On the contrary. They are also the beginning of a state or an action; through language, one gains access, one evokes, one creates a world in which spirituality and music can meet, can be related, can perhaps even coalesce.[13]

Simultaneously with their own self-effacement, the presented preludes *produce* music, spirituality and their interrelations, as exteriorities thereby invading and infecting the interior and displacing the opposition. The foreplays become the play itself.[14]

---

[11]   Another word that comes to my mind here is *paratext*, a term coined by Gérard Genette in the late 1980s. Paratextual elements like titles, prefaces, footnotes, tables of contents, and so on are always pointing in two directions, encouraging readers on one hand to look more intently at the 'main' text (the paratext is destined to be completed by the reading of the 'main' text), but also to look away from it toward other 'texts.' Paratextuality thus simultaneously makes and unmakes textual unity.

[12]   The *pro*gram as pro*gram*, as Derrida writes (Derrida 1981a: 20).

[13]   Words bring up what was unarticulated before. They make it possible for something to emerge in the first place. Here I am especially referring to words that do not (re)present something tangible or comprehensible but that try to refer to unthought-of dimensions, unsettled zones that escape common thinking, an effort to orientate towards the unthinkable, although it should be clear that this can never be more than a provisional and tentative approximation.

[14]   Maurice Blanchot calls this the 'paradox of desperation,' the impossible position of somebody who finds himself in a domain far beyond the sayable but who nevertheless feels the urgent need to speak from that position (see Blanchot 1999). He has to write and not-write simultaneously. The problem of writing is not the 'adequate expression,' the attempt to describe something in ever more accurate terms, something an author has clearly in mind but which is waiting for an exact translation. The problem is, first, that there is no 'adequate expression' and, second, that there is even no original something. Writing thus becomes an absolute impossibility: it tries to translate something that does not exist.

I found the inspiration for this remark in Patricia de Martelaere's *Een verlangen naar ontroostbaarheid* [A Longing to be Inconsolable] (1994: 20).

THRESHOLD 3
Stories

W HY would someone feel compelled to write a book on music and spirituality? No. Stop! This question must be rephrased immediately. Why would *I* wish to write a book on music and spirituality? What is this inner drive, this almost compulsive urge, to reveal to you, to let you share in (in Dutch as well as German both meanings resonate in the words 'mededelen' and 'mitteilen' respectively) my pools of thought, albeit far from being systematically organized or comprehensive, concerning this subject? Where does *my* fascination with the relation between music and spirituality come from? Fascination, that is, according to the *OED*, a deprivation of the power of escape or resistance. I offer here four stations, four quite dissimilar leads. Four personal anchorages, from religion to literature and from film to faith, should serve here as a kind of justification.

First station. I was already exposed, early in my childhood, to what could be called the supernatural powers of music. As a little boy I sat, wedged between my parents, in one of the front rows of our Catholic church in a small village in the South of the Netherlands, listening to the priest reading Joshua 6, the conquest of Jericho by the Israelites. Of course, what strikes you as a kid is the murderous military campaign under the leadership of Joshua, the successor to Moses. Leaving deep marks of violence, Joshua and the Israelites traverse the Promised Land, disposing of the original inhabitants: men, women, children, and animals are killed, cities are reduced to ashes.[1]

However, what particularly fascinated me in this story was the way by which the Israelites conquered Jericho.[2] Thick walls protected the mighty city against possible intruders and aggressors. But this is what God said to Joshua:

> You shall march around the city, all the men of war circling the city once. You shall do so for six days. Also seven priests shall carry seven trumpets of ram's horns before the ark; then on the seventh day you shall march around the city seven times, and the priests shall blow the trumpets. It shall be that when they make a long blast with the ram's horn, and when you hear the sound of the trumpet, all the people shall shout with a great shout; and the wall of the city will fall down flat, and the people will go up every man straight ahead. (Joshua 6:3–5)

---

[1]   Already from its early beginning, Christianity seems predicated upon the expulsion of the 'other.' So doing, Joshua and his comrades are anticipating the ancient Greek practice of dividing the world into 'humans' and 'barbarians.' And this very binary division into pure and impure is in all cases dialectically tied to a repressed 'primal scene' of violent expulsion and purgation (Kearney 2002: 86).

[2]   Contrasting sharply with what perhaps could be considered as one of the first documented ethnical cleansings in the world's history – I might recall Walter Benjamin's phrase here that every document of civilization is written over a tale of barbarism – is the rather cheerful melody of the Negro spiritual 'Joshua Fit de Battle ob Jerico.'

This was done accordingly, and the blasts of the seven *shofars* and the accompanying din of the people sufficed to destroy this putatively impregnable fortress.[3]

Through music God plays his power, and the power is vested in the music.[4] Was it the number of decibels that made the walls collapse? Should this devastating material effect of sound be ascribed to so-called 'forced resonance'?[5] Or should we turn to Godwin who suggests a more transcendental and metaphysical 'explanation' (see footnote 3)? I am not looking for an exhaustive answer here, nor is this book designed to deconstruct these kinds of myths in favor of more or less rational explanations and scientific disentanglements (which themselves are, to a certain extent, myths – myths are, after all, nothing more and nothing less than stories

---

[3]   An opposite development takes place in the myth of Amphion and Zethus. Amphion and his twin brother Zethus, illegitimate sons of Zeus and Antiope, are exposed as infants, but survive. Meeting their mother when they are fully grown, they avenge her as she has been kept as a slave by Lycus, the ruler of Thebes, and his wife Dirce, and take power in the city by force, killing the royal couple. Amphion then becomes king of Thebes, and as the city has no ramparts yet, the brothers decide to build them. Zethus, from childhood fond of manual work and tilling the soil, carries many stones from far and wide to Thebes. He reproaches Amphion, who has dedicated himself to music since receiving a lyre from Hermes, for not being of much help. Whereupon Amphion takes his lyre and starts singing. The (mythical) music causes the stones to roll and assemble themselves into towers. According to musicologist Joscelyn Godwin, the insight at the core of this myth is "that Nature is ultimately responsible not to the common-sensible laws of cause and effect which seem to rule the material world, but to transcendent principles which have a perpetual existence in a higher order of being" (Godwin 1987: 13). This explanation makes the spiritual powers of music in this myth all the more evident.

[4]   Tracing music's supernatural powers in the Bible also leads to King Saul and his servant David (see 1 Samuel 16–19). King Saul is periodically haunted by evil spirits. His servants advise him to seek a man who is skillful on the harp, telling him "it shall come about when the evil spirit from God is on you, that he shall play the harp with his hand, and you will be well." Saul acts on their advice and finally traces David, recommended as 'a skillful musician.' This is how the story proceeds in the book Samuel: "So it came about whenever the evil spirit from God came to Saul, David would take the harp and play it with his hand; and Saul would be refreshed and be well, and the evil spirit would depart from him" (1 Samuel 16:23). The music, however, cannot cure Saul completely. David's success as a warrior makes Saul furious and three times he tries to kill David with a spear while David is playing the harp. But at each attempt, Saul's weapon misses David. Isn't it, in light of the preceding, conceivable that (David's) music acts as an invisible protective shield? That music is a manifestation of some divine power, able to protect the innocent and righteous? That music and spirituality are natural allies?

[5]   Forced resonance is the effect that occurs when the resonance of certain sounds matches the natural frequency of an object, thereby setting the bonds of the object into motion. When the energy of the sound waves excessively vacillates the natural frequency of an object, the object can rupture. A beautiful example can be found in Günther Grass's novel *Die Blechtrommel* [The Tin Drum], when Oskar discovers how his high shrieking can make glass objects crack. This screaming turns out to be his ultimate weapon to prevent people from taking away his drum.

people tell themselves in order to explain how the world came to be).[6] Rather, I am chiefly interested in the working of these archaic stories,[7] how they affected (and still affect) me and how they function in creating a relationship between an aural culture (or, more specifically, music) and spirituality.[8] I am interested as to how these parables also constitute a discourse on music's spiritual powers which is permeated by or even founded on divinity, the supernatural, and otherworldliness. In my opinion, these narratives also influence to this very day the preconceptions

---

[6]   This being said, I do not intend to treat fictional and non-fictional narratives equally, although the difference between fact and fiction is often blurry as Sigmund Freud and Hayden White, for example, suggest in their writings. Freud concedes that his psycho-analytic interpretations might have as much to do with 'narratives' as with 'facts.' For Hayden White, a historian does not merely tell a story. He shapes an entire set of events, considered as a completed whole, into a story. In *Serendipities*, Umberto Eco warns us for the construction of an ontological distinction between stories and facts: "Recognizing that our history was inspired by many tales we now recognize as false should make us alert, ready to call constantly into question the very tales we believe true" (Eco 1999: 26).

In *On Stories*, philosopher Richard Kearney further elaborates on the relation between historical narratives and fictional ones, concluding that they often overlap. While there is always a certain fictionality to our representing history 'as if' we were actually there in the past to experience it, we can recognize, by the same token, a certain historical character to fictional narratives – for example the fact that most stories are recounted in the past tense and describe characters and events as though they were real (Kearney 2002: 143). Kearney finds an ally in Paul Ricoeur, who states that history is both a literary artifact as well as a representation of reality. However, Kearney does not go so far as to state that fact and fiction can never be, at least partially, disentangled and distinguished (Kearney 2002: 37).

I only want to assert here that myths, just like fairy tales, literature, and scientific treatises affect our ideas on spirituality and its relation to music. Not infrequently, fictional stories seem quite plausible, sometimes more than everyday reality, which is far more complex and less credible. Stories seem to explain something that is otherwise hard to understand.

[7]   Christian religion is explicitly based on narrative testimony, see, for example, Luke 1:1–4:

Since many have undertaken to compile a narrative of the events that have been fulfilled among us, just as those who were eyewitnesses from the beginning and ministers of the word have handed them down to us, I too have decided, after investigating everything accurately anew, to write it down in an orderly sequence for you, most excellent Theophilus, so that you may realize the certainty of the teachings you have reached.

[8]   In this respect, an observation of British philosopher David Hartley (1705–57) might be relevant. In his principal work *Observations on Man, his Frame, his Duty, and his Expectations* from 1749 he writes that the ear is of much more importance to us, considered as spiritual beings, than the eye, a remark with a more than faint echo of the deeply Pauline conviction that faith comes through hearing. More than two centuries later, Marshall McLuhan resumes this idea, albeit in a pejorative way. McLuhan creates a hierarchically organized binary opposition in which the 'ear culture' – equated with a magical and timeless world – is subordinate to the objective and progressive 'world of the eye.'

through which we assess the bond between music and the spiritual. In any case, they engage experiences of extremity, residing at the edge of our conventional understanding, and seek to address phenomena beyond the strict frontiers of reason alone; they are efforts in new possibilities of saying and being. Abiding conviction that when we are confronted with the apparently inexplicable and unthinkable, narratives matter (Kearney 2002: 157).

Second station. Soon after its publication in 1993, I read Helmut Krausser's bestseller *Melodien* [Melodies]. Rereading it recently, I do not consider it a particularly interesting book. However, I remember that I was somehow fascinated by it, especially in the period immediately following my studies as a jazz pianist at the Conservatory of Rotterdam. When becoming a professionally trained musician led me to the experience that somewhere in that process my love for music had severely decreased, it was through reading literature – this literature – that the love suddenly revived, precisely because of the enigmatic but strong powers which were attributed to music.

In *Melodien*, the sixteenth-century Florentine alchemist Castiglio is in pursuit of the essence of music. He makes several attempts to penetrate its secrets, as he believes that they enclose a wealth of earthly power; after all, music, more than anything else, has the power to manipulate and change man's moods.[9] Castiglio thinks of

---

[9]   A more current and secular example, testifying to the recognition of music's manipulating powers, can be found in Frank Zappa's musical triptych *Joe's Garage* (1979) which tells the story of how Joe and some other characters are driven to certain crimes (from noise pollution to sexual perversities) by that "horrible force called music." The government finally decides to make music – the prime cause of unwanted mass behavior – illegal in order to be better able to control its citizens. From that moment on, Joe can only dream imaginary guitar notes. In a short comment in the CD leaflet, Zappa writes: "If the plot of the story seems just a little bit preposterous [...] just be glad you don't live in one of the cheerful little countries where, at this very moment, music is either severely restricted or [...] totally illegal." In 1979, Zappa, with this last remark, referred to Iran. In 2005, Iranian Prime Minister Mahmoud Ahmadinejad tried to reinstall this ban on Western music. And, 24 years after Zappa's release, music historian Richard Taruskin writes in the *New York Times* about the abolition of music during the Taliban regime in Afghanistan: "The only sounds on the Taliban-dominated radio that Western ears would recognize as musical were those of ritual chanting (something quite distinct from 'music,' both conceptually and linguistically, in Islamic thought as in many of the world's cultures)" (Taruskin 2001). In the end, Taruskin somehow seems to understand the Taliban's contention with music. Music is not blameless, he writes; it can inflict harm. The Taliban know that, and it is about time that the Western world learns this too. The impact music has on the consciousness and subconscious of humans should not be underestimated, according to Taruskin. In that sense, he too stands in an old and influential tradition that attributes supernatural and transcendent powers to music, a tradition that can also be recognized in many interpretations connecting Mozart's *Zauberflöte* to Freemasonry. If the main theme of *Die Zauberflöte* can be described as a 'transformation' or 'initiation' – primarily Tamino and Pamina must endure several ordeals to become initiated in the secrets of Isis and Osiris – it is the music itself that is presented

music as a divine language and dreams of discovering the rules to which it adheres in order to systematically construct melodies that summon a deep enchantment; he is looking for the musical stone tablets of the law, a complete translation of the *vox dei* which would enable one to create a music wielding almost hypnotic powers. Castiglio's ambition is to apply these celestial sounds to the welfare of the human race. In the end, he 'finds' 26 magic melodies, so-called *tropoi*, able to cheer up the depressed, to cure the sick, and to cause people to fall in love.

Of course, especially as a musician, one becomes curious as to how these *tropoi* sound. This desire, however, remains unfulfilled; in the course of the narrative, the melodies become lost. (Only very faint reflections of them are traceable in the music of Palestrina, Gesualdo, the castrato Antonio Pasqualini, and, most of all, in Allegri's *Miserere*).[10] However, Krausser does present the reader with an 'authentic source' in the person of Castiglio's servant, Andrea, who attempts to describe the *tropoi*. No simple task, as they do not resemble any music known at that time. The first hint is that the melodies (of course) consist of tone sequences and are therefore not distinguishable, superficially, from other sequences. It is essentially a frequent repetition which imbues them with something sweeping and magical: only after twelve repetitions does their working expand (Krausser 1993: 194 and 202).

The ultimate melodies are 'out of tune,' incoherent, disharmonious, constantly unresolved, full of shifts and alterations, "a haphazard up and down stuff – huge intervals which don't make any sense," according to Andrea. No intrinsic order can be discovered. Familiar changes make way for complex and unexpected cadences; yet, every tone seems to follow the previous one in a logical way. The experiences it induces in Andrea are permanently vacillating between goose bumps and curiosity, pain and pleasure, fascination and repugnance; the *tropoi* are heavenly and diabolical at the same time, inducing both fear and delight, *Lust* and *Unlust* (Krausser 1993: 230 and 283).

Sacred or spiritual music, untranslatable into and irreducible to current conventions, escaping the laws of compositional constructions and evoking a sense of infinity through its abundant repetitions – this music incites a listening

---

as the most important transformative power from darkness to light. The subject of Mozart's last opera is the transcendent powers of music. Music creates here its own mythos. (See for a detailed study, Tjeu van den Berk's *The Magic Flute: An Alchemical Allegory* [Leiden: Brill, 2004].)

10   The search for the *tropoi* in Krausser's novel remarkably resemble the attempt of modern scholars and musicians to reconstruct the 'magical songs' of the fifteenth-century Florentine philosopher Marsilio Ficino. Ficino was fascinated by the healing effects *magi* like Hermes Trismegistus, Orpheus, Pythagoras, and Plato reputedly achieved through song and incantation, notably the ability to cure diseases of the soul and body, to expel evil passions, and to bring the soul into a state of virtuous harmony. Ficino had no idea what this ancient music had sounded like, but he tried to reconstruct their spiritual songs. Contemporary scholars have to face the same difficulties: no examples of original instruments, musical notation, or traces of the sounds themselves remain (Gouk 2004: 100–101).

in which an interweaving of two radically opposed emotional responses takes place, outside of the subject-centered infrastructure of 'ordinary' experience. The spiritual powers attributed to music by Castiglio and the feelings it evokes seem a blueprint of what philosophers like Immanuel Kant and Edmund Burke in the eighteenth century, and Jean-François Lyotard in the twentieth century regarded as the sublime in or aroused by certain artworks. The unearthly powers of music, according to Krausser, encapsulated in the 26 *tropoi*, seem at least to be a religious version of the more secularized concept of the sublime.[11] In the continuation of this book, I wish to run this gauntlet and circumscribe the concept of spirituality in terms quite closely related to contemporary thinking on the sublime. However, an important departure with Kant's reading of the sublime will be that I do not consider spirituality as a purely subjective phenomenon which (by appealing to Reason) contributes to the elevation of that very subject. Neither will I completely follow Lyotard's suggestions concerning the sublime and regard spirituality as a (possible) characteristic of (certain) music.[12] Spirituality should not, in my opinion, be situated in the object (music); instead, I see it primarily as a rupture in our relation with the object, a break in our perception. Or, to be more precise, spirituality is neither subjective nor objective: it takes place in the space between

---

[11]   In *Das Heilige* [*The Idea of the Holy*], Rudolf Otto recognizes an affinity between a sublime feeling and a feeling of the spiritual. According to Otto, the aesthetical sublime should be regarded as a later development or a weak representation of a more original, irreducible, and unparalleled feeling of what he calls 'the numinous' (see also Threshold 6).

[12]   In 'After the Sublime, the State of Aesthetics,' Lyotard (implicitly) recognizes the sublime in many modern musical works, ranging from Debussy to Cage and from Webern to Boulez. As Lyotard is primarily in discussion with Kant, he of course knows very well how Kant's notion of the sublime settles scores with the idea that the sublime can be (re)presented in or by an object. In order to save an aesthetical sublime, that is, a sublime somehow perceivable by the senses, Lyotard thus cannot resort to the form of an artwork. As an alternative, against or beyond Kant, he proposes to seek the sublime in matter, in the (mere) materiality of a work. With that, Lyotard's contemplations are not going in the direction of what matter can tell us once we reflect on it and submit it to our thinking. On the contrary: he is advocating an attitude capable of suspending the activity of comparing and grasping, those acts of aggression that are of the regime of the mind. Lyotard points at 'a mindless state of mind, which is required of the mind not for matter to be perceived or conceived, given or grasped,' a pre-reflective state in one of the dispositions of sensibility through which 'mind is accessible to the material event, can be "touched" by it: a singular, incomparable quality – unforgettable and immediately forgotten – of [...] a timbre or a nuance' (Lyotard 1991: 140–42). The matter thus invoked is something that is not destined; it is 'presence as unpresentable to the mind, always withdrawn from its grasp' (Lyotard 1991: 142).

Although Lyotard here skids along a twentieth-century formalism which I would like to avoid, I embrace the further interpretation he gives of the sublime as it touches on my ideas concerning spirituality. (For a more elaborate discussion of Lyotard's thoughts in relation to spirituality, see Threshold 10.)

subject and object; it comes into being in relations, relations stripped off from ordinary structures.

Already having said too much, too impetuously, too precipitously, I interrupt these thoughts here now, as the only aim of this chapter was to uncover some motives behind this book, to get to know its scriptor to some extent.[13] So, let's continue the acquaintance.

Third station. How music affects animals is shown beautifully in the semi-documentary I saw some time ago, *The Story of the Weeping Camel* (2003) by Byambasuren Davaa and Luigi Falorni, an enchanting tale of a family of herders in Mongolia's Gobi desert who face a crisis when a mother camel rejects her newborn colt after an excruciatingly difficult delivery.[14] Without its mother's

---

[13] I am deliberately using the word 'scriptor' instead of 'author' here, referring to the well-known text by Roland Barthes 'The Death of the Author.' "The author is never more than the instance writing, just as I is nothing other than the instance saying I," Barthes writes (Barthes 1977: 145). Thus, where the author (Barthes writes a capital 'A' here, presenting him as a transcendental signified) is the past of his own book, the modern scriptor is born simultaneously with the text, and whose only power is to (re)mix writings.

So the instance writing 'I' here is a construct, a discursive product, never able to control 'his' texts nor to act as their origin. Nevertheless, 'I' try to attest to certain events that (temporarily) relate me in a unique way to the topic under discussion. In that sense, there is also a space between an individual being and his discursive (re)presentation.

[14] The influence of music on animals is also portrayed in Western cultural artifacts. One famous story is *The Pied Piper of Hamelin* (1842), a children's poem by Robert Browning based on some obscure historical event that occurred in the North German town of Hameln in 1284. Hameln is suffering from a terrible plague of rats. The town council tries everything to get rid of them, without success. At last, the Mayor promises a thousand florins to the one who can put an end to the plague. At that juncture, a stranger shows up and says he can rid Hameln of the vermin. How? By playing his magic flute. This is how Browning describes what happens:

> Into the street the Piper stepped, smiling first a little smile. As if he knew what magic slept, in his quiet pipe the while. Then, like a musical adept, to blow the pipe his lips he wrinkled. And green and blue his sharp eyes twinkled, like a candle-flame where salt is sprinkled. And ere three shrill notes the pipe uttered, you heard as if an army muttered. And the muttering grew to a grumbling; and the grumbling grew to a mighty rumbling. And out of the houses the rats came tumbling.

The pied piper leads them towards the river Weser, where they drown, all except one. To other rats, this one survivor tells how the music enchanted them: "At the first shrill notes of the pipe, I heard a sound as of scraping tripe, and putting apples, wondrous ripe, into a cider-press's gripe." The music, twice described as 'shrill,' is able to bewitch the rats completely, without a significant influence on humans. (Later on this changes. When the Mayor refuses to pay the fee – playing a tune on a flute is not worth a thousand florins, he grudges – the piper returns. Again, he starts to play a tune on his flute – "such sweet soft notes as yet musician's cunning never gave the enraptured air." This time, all the children

milk, the (rare white) little camel will not survive. So, after other failed attempts and in accordance with an ancient ritual, a musician is finally summoned from a backwater town to perform a ceremony that is meant to coax the mother into nursing her baby.[15] While he plays his *Morin Huur*, a female herder sings a song and soothingly rubs the mother camel's belly. After a while (in the movie it is only a couple of minutes, in reality it lasted almost a day), the mother spreads her hind legs, thereby allowing the colt to search for her udder. While the baby greedily drinks, tears begin to fall from the mother's eyes, the ultimate sign that she finally accepts her newborn.

The *Hoosh* rite that is recounted here is an age-old custom still evident in present-day Mongolia, where shepherds connect their satellite television sets to solar panels but also where a good musician and the whispering of some magic words can offer a better cure for their cattle than a visit to a veterinarian. For these nomads, the result of the *Hoosh* rite is no small wonder – according to the herders it can take a while but it never fails – but little more than an ancient method whose worth is proven by now, a normal part of a cultural tradition, albeit a culture under attack from Western influences. The magical radiation of the music is taken for granted, nothing mysterious, not even worth mentioning. It is us, Westerners, who have lost much of our contact with the spiritual possibilities of music, who come in large numbers to movie theaters to gape at these incredible events.

Should we conclude from this story – a story that 'alters' us by transporting us to another place where we can experience things otherwise – that the spiritual powers of music are no placebo effect, no sheer manipulation of a human mind, when even animals are influenced by it? Is this event grist to the mill of those who take the position that the relation between spirituality and music can be re-traced to some specific formalistic characteristics of that music (see Threshold 4)? Or does *The Story of the Weeping Camel* make manifest the idea that our Western thinking, our logocentrism as Derrida calls it, cannot withstand such occurrences? Could a possible but uncomfortable conclusion be that this story breaks with the customary concepts, truths, and beliefs of Western rationality, explanation models, and logic, just like that 'certain Chinese encyclopedia' cited in a text by Borges, which too deconstructs all the ordered surfaces of our thoughts and confronts us with their limitations?[16] And is it exactly there, in that non-localizable space (non-localizable

---

follow him, without ever returning to Hameln again. A kind of epilogue states that at the place of the children's retreat it was and still is forbidden for anyone to play music. Music has turned from an eliminator of animal inconvenience into an instrument of eternal loss and separation, of violence against children, an aural nightmare for parents.)

[15]   As the elder members of the family recognize the seriousness of the case, they insist on searching for not just any musician, but a particularly good one.

[16]   The encyclopedia presented by Borges divides animals into the following categories: a) belonging to the Emperor, b) embalmed, c) tame, d) sucking pigs, e) sirens, f) fabulous, g) stray dogs, h) included in the present classification, i) frenzied, j) innumerable, k) drawn with a very fine camelhair brush, l) *et cetera*, m) having just broken the water pitcher, n) that

because what is inscribed here is the occurrence of a thought as the unthought that remains to be thought in the decline of Western thinking) that spirituality and music meet, perform their power, display their strength?[17] In this book, I will primarily investigate this last question, which implies that I will argue against the view that certain music can be adorned with the label 'spiritual' on the basis of intrinsic qualities.[18]

Fourth station. This book is partly the result of a struggle with my religious past,[19] that is, a past in which the institution Church played a weighty role. In this past, religion and music were often inextricably connected: first as a member of the church's children's choir, later as its organ player, music-making for me took place mainly in church. (Furthermore, the songs I sang at home or learned at the Catholic primary school often had religious texts as well. One could also argue as to what extent the daily repetition of saying one's prayers has a musical

from a long way off look like flies. Michel Foucault opens his book *Les mots et les choses* [*The Order of Things*] with the wonderment of this taxonomy: "The thing we apprehend in one great leap, the thing that, by means of the fable, is demonstrated as the exotic charm of another system of thought, is the limitation of our own, the stark impossibility of thinking *that*" (Foucault 1971: xv).

[17] "For those of us who enjoy the mixed blessing of seeing beyond all traditions and thus finding ourselves without an anchor in the world, spirituality is rather an arduous process, filled with doubts and misgivings, skeptical of glib formulations and platitudes," Robert C. Solomon writes in *Spirituality for the Skeptic* (Solomon 2002: 140). Though I am not adhering to his main ideas on a so-called 'naturalized spirituality,' I am sympathetic towards his thought that spirituality should embrace the material world. According to Solomon, spirituality (and he immediately adds: like music) is a celebration of life. Spirituality regarded as something supernatural too readily projects it away from us. It would be a mistake to take this concept in out-of-this-world terms, Solomon writes. He shows himself as a follower of Nietzsche. Nietzsche defends a robust, this-world spirituality and rejects the nay-saying of otherworldly thinkers (beginning with Socrates), who put all their cards on an eternal life instead of a mere earthly one. In some way or another, I consider myself part of this critical tradition.

[18] I will try to present several reasons for my decision not to follow this common line of thought. Here, I would like to mention a book by Gilbert Rouget called *La musique et la transe* (*Music and Trance*) (1985). In it, Rouget concludes that no universal law can explain the relations between music and spiritual experiences such as trance; they vary greatly and depend on the system of meanings within their cultural context. Forcefully rejecting pseudo-science and reductionism, Rouget demystifies theories of the intrinsic magical powers of music, the neurophysiological effects of drumming on trance, and the idea that square rhythms do not have any hypnotic effect. He concludes that music's physiological and emotional effects are inseparable from patterns of collective representations and behavior, and that music and trance are linked in as many ways as there are cultural structures. Often, the role of music is much less to produce a trance than to create conditions favorable to its onset; music does nothing more than socialize trance, enabling it to fully develop.

[19] "You talk to me of nationality, language, religion. I shall try to fly by those nets," Stephen Daedalus retorts in James Joyce's *Portrait of the Artist as a Young Man*.

component. Especially the chaplet, with its constantly recurring Hail Maries, often led me to a state of perpetuation in which the words lost all their meaning in favor of some rhythmic pattern closely resembling the drone of certain minimal music. Though the tone, timbre, and rhythm of this *Sprechgesang* thus almost entirely 'drowned out' the religious content, the chaplet retained its religious meaning on a non-discursive, trance-like level.)

As for many Dutch, growing up in the 1960s and '70s, my teenage period was characterized by an opposition to and a slow breaking away from the galling bonds of institutionalized religion.[20] However, this never resulted in a complete relinquishing of a curiosity for religious and/or spiritual events.[21] In this sense, I recognize myself in the struggle with religion and the Church described by Gianni Vattimo in *Credere di credere* [*Belief*]. In a philosophically grounded credo, Vattimo claims that a dogmatic and disciplining Christianity has nothing to do with a religion or a spirituality he is seeking (again). The menacing but simultaneously reassuring doctrine of the Church is not able to call him back or to appeal to him. Retrieving faith for Vattimo means reconsidering the import of the Christian Revelation in secularized terms, which also means taking into account the historical context of our time: "Christ's message does not resound in empty space but rather sets a task with respect to the situation in which we find ourselves," Vattimo writes (Vattimo 1999: 80). To give this flesh and blood, Vattimo rejects the image of a God which contains all characteristics of omnipotence, absoluteness, eternity, and transcendence, calling them "projections of human desires," meant only to enable oneself to depend upon a Supreme Being (Vattimo 1999: 38).[22] It is precisely the

---

[20]   I learned much later how Martin Heidegger had to shake off the yoke of what he called 'the system of Catholicism' in the 1920s. His philosophical quest brought him to the point where he could no longer believe according to the escape routes of comforting metaphysical constructions. Against this, Heidegger conceptualizes *das faktische Leben* (a factical life) that falls into a void and which should regard God as the fundamentally unknown instead of a humanized identity. Heidegger discards the reliance on faith as a betrayal of truth. In the place of long-established truth dogmas, he advocates a metaphysical homelessness. Let's just say I feel at home in this sphere of homelessness.

[21]   In the late 1980s, I frequented several so-called New Age groups, and for a short while became a member of what has in the past been labeled a sect, where we learned to read the Bible according to cabbalistic insights. In these groups, music usually functioned as a tool for relaxation and dissociation from everyday life. Though most music played at the sessions was tranquil, tensionless, harmonic, slow, and soft, we sometimes danced or performed physically heavy exercises to up-tempo, rhythmic, arousing tunes, that almost brought the participants into a state of trance. Also community singing ("*I am* my sunshine, my only sunshine, *I* make me happy, when skies are grey") was a recurrent part of those meetings, creating a sense of belonging, a musically-constructed and safe inside precariously able to preclude the evil outside world. In other words, control over the aural environment was an important aspect of those meetings in order to create the desired atmosphere.

[22]   In *The Wisdom of Insecurity*, theologian Alan W. Watts 'defines' God as that which remains undefinable, the unknown reality. In assent, he cites the Hindu *Upanishads*, saying: "He who thinks that God is not comprehended, by him God is comprehended; but he who

process of secularization which provides a liberation of human reason from its dependence upon an absolute God thought of as a fearful Judge presenting himself as both transcendent and capricious. In other words, secularization has a cleansing effect on believing; it is a positive fact within the Christian tradition as it makes it possible to deal with the absolutization of some contingent historical values and perspectives, and it gets even with the extreme literalism in the interpretation of dogmas and precepts. Regarded this way, the process of secularization is a blessing for belief, religion, and spirituality.

What appeals to Vattimo is the rigor of a post-metaphysical discourse that is born of the effort required to cultivate an attitude of persuasion without proclaiming ideas of universality or neutrality. According to him, contemporary (continental) philosophy has become aware of the implicit violence intrinsic to every finality, every closure, and every principle that silences all further questioning. Taking this insight into account, his ideas on religion and spirituality are not rocks of eternally assigned tenets to which we can turn in order to be on solid ground in this era of insecurity and heterogeneity (Vattimo 1999: 65).[23]

Are Vattimo's thoughts somehow consoling? I find them at least relieving (though none too original) in the sense that they can serve as a confirmation that spirituality does not necessarily belong to (an) organized religion; there is also a home for it outside the domains of the world's established religions (though by this I do not at all wish to say that spirituality cannot exist in institutionalized religious practices).

However, I am fully aware that the insight to be drawn from *Belief*, that spirituality is a floating concept – floating because of its historical contingency – not providing firm ground, but rather questioning every stabilization, every hiding within established ways of thinking, is far less soothing. Nevertheless, this is the path I want to, I *must* walk. This is the space I need to explore – an empty space, no longer inhabited by the God presented to me in my childhood by priests, teachers, and parents. How, after 'the Death of God,' to give the still valuable concept of spirituality a meaningful interpretation – that is what kept and keeps me occupied during this journey we call 'life.'

What is the role of music in all this? According to Jacques Attali, music is – or at least was – a strategy running parallel to religion. Primordially, music as well as religion has as its function the creation, legitimation, and maintenance of order. Its primary purpose is not to be sought in aesthetics, which is a modern invention, but in the effectiveness of its participation in social regulation. Both music and religion honor harmony and are produced to make people believe, to believe in

---

thinks that God is comprehended knows him not. God is unknown to those who know him, and is known to those who do not know him at all" (Watts 1951: 150).

[23] "From tender youth we are told by father and teacher that betrayal is the most heinous offense imaginable. But what is betrayal? Betrayal means breaking ranks, going off into the unknown," Milan Kundera writes in *The Unbearable Lightness of Being*.

order: "When the rites and music are clear and complete, heaven and earth fulfill their normal functions" (Attali 1985: 60).

This is, however, only one aspect of the role music plays in society. Music has another facet as well, a dark side, marked by subversion and ambivalence. For Attali, music is always already permeated by noise, that is, internal and external powers that threaten and finally undermine the existing (musical) order. In the end, Attali foresees a music that reflects an open, unstable history, a production of music that will help us enter a realm of 'fantastic insecurity' (Attali 1985: 146).

In my opinion, it is in this realm of fantastic insecurity that music and spirituality meet. What I would like to reveal in the next pages, the next thresholds, is how music is able to instigate a rethinking of the spiritual and how this new, de- and reterritorialized concept of spirituality opens up new possibilities to encounter music. To ruminate how spirituality sets itself to work in or through music might open an other space where music can dwell, develop, and be received. Dwelling in this space that is both created by and allowing of reflection becomes simultaneously the act of transforming it, adding on, replacing, altering, transgressing the already existing limits: never fully defined but always in the process of being defined.

THRESHOLD 4
New Spiritual Music

THIS book finds its cause in the Festival *Nieuwe spirituele muziek* (New Spiritual Music), held November, 1999 in Amsterdam and for which there was a continuation in June, 2007.[1] New Spiritual Music. "The last big movement in the development of the music history of the 20th century that simultaneously marks the transition towards the 21st century," read the program notes.[2] They continue: "If only because of the very essential change in the aesthetic and cultural-philosophical foundations of the New Spiritual Music with respect to the traditional avant-garde since World War II, the aggravated attention that the composers of spiritual music will receive during this large-scale festival is justified."

The organizers of the festival speak decisively of a movement. Although this movement is quite diverse, various music theorists, musicologists, journalists, composers, and musicians attempted to delineate some binding factors; like always, a new movement needs to be separated from other styles and genres, other schools, both diachronically and synchronically. It needs to be identified, that is, invested with an identity,[3] in order to come into existence.[4] It must possess and be possessed by a name.[5]

----

[1]   With reference to footnote 3 in Threshold 2, I consider my text a *para*text (against or besides the text) rather than a *meta*text (a comment on an already existing other text). I feel a certain affinity with the contribution of the famous artist Joseph Kosuth to the so-called *Xerox Book* (1968), creating paratexts that will always already be the main text.

[2]   All translations of the program notes are mine.

[3]   Identity can be defined as the sameness of a thing at all times or in all circumstances. In other words, it refers to the condition or fact that a thing is itself and not something else.

[4]   I will defer for a while elaborating on the problematical sides of creating a movement. My observations stem not so much from a sociological or organizational point of view, but, primarily, from an aesthetic perspective: lumping artworks together makes the unequal equal. The proclamation of a new school is certainly not always for the sake of the artworks. Often, reasons of cultural policy are at stake.

[5]   What I am pointing out here is the institutionalization, regulation, and disciplining of 'the spiritual.' There is a remarkable similarity with the term 'mystic' at the close of the Middle Ages, as analyzed by Michel de Certeau:

At first it is an adjective: it is added, as if to designate a specific usage, to noun units already constituted by language. It designates 'ways of doing' or 'ways of saying,' ways of using the language. Little by little, these adjectival usages, becoming more complex and more explicit, were grouped within a domain of their own, their specific designation identified, toward the end of the 16th century, by the noun form: 'la mystique.' The nominal form marked the will to unify all these operations, hitherto dispersed, that were to be coordinated, selected (what is truly 'mystical'?), and regulated under the heading of a *modus loquendi* ('a manner of speaking'). Thus the word no longer modeled itself, as the adjective had done, on the noun units of one sole great ('biblical') Narration in order to connote the many spiritual appropriations or interiorizations of the biblical text. It became a text itself ... Once it had become substantivized into a noun, *mystics* had to determine its procedures and define its

Of course, when the time has come, we need to examine more carefully the 'newness' of this movement. How is it, for example, different, perhaps even opposed to the spiritual music that is, with the stroke of this one predicate, declared 'old'? However, let us first pursue our explorations by concentrating on that other, more important adjective: 'spiritual.'

What are the main characteristics of New Spiritual Music, announced in a Dutch TV program as "the solution for the crisis in contemporary classical music"? In other words, what exactly is meant by this "change in the aesthetic and cultural-philosophical foundations"? The festival program notes quote a Dutch composer/critic: "This so-called spiritual music is part of a much larger complex, that is, the departure from classical modernism." In almost all respects, the musical principles of the New Spiritual Music seem to be diametrically opposed to those of modernism: repetition and rest versus development and progress, tradition and recognizability versus innovation and experiment, communication versus individualism and conceptualism, tonality versus atonality, intuitive simplicity versus academic complexity, spiritual narrations versus rational abstractions – also reasons why this music can adorn itself with the title 'New Euphony.' Customarily, Estonian composer Arvo Pärt is mentioned as the founder; his change from composing music "based on experiments" to music "based on communication, religion, and emotion" also marks, retrospectively, the transition from modernistic to spiritual music.[6]

Modern Western societies have fallen victim to the dominance of exploitation and calculation, a strong craving for control and the expulsion of incomprehensible phenomena. Culture has become an industry; the world is disenchanted. The toll the West has to pay to embrace this modernity is the obstruction of entry to the spiritual, so the argumentation goes. Within this reasoning, a watershed is occurring, a schism, a cleavage. The return of spirituality in music is simultaneously presented as the farewell to modernity, to modern or avant-garde music. The New Spiritual Music movement separates Arnold Schönberg from Arvo Pärt, Pierre Boulez from John Tavener, Karl-Heinz Stockhausen from Giya Kancheli because it advocates and propagates a musical language that renounces most attainments of serialism and dodecaphonism. The 'new' magic words are 'tonality,' 'triads,' and 'repetition.' Titles like *Passion* (Erkki-Sven Tüür,

---

object. Although [...] it succeeded in carrying out the first part of this program, the second part was to prove impossible. Is not its object infinite? It is never anything but the unstable metaphor for what is inaccessible ... *Mystics* only assembles and orders its practices in the name of something that it cannot make into an object (unless it be a mystical one), something that never ceases judging *mystics* at the same time that it eludes it. Mysticism vanished at its point of origin. Its birth pledges it to the impossible, as if, stricken by the absolute from the very beginning, it finally died of the question from which it was formed. (De Certeau 1992: 77)

[6]   The quotes are taken from an interview with one of the programmers which appeared in a Dutch daily.

Estonia), *Magnificat* (Joep Franssens, the Netherlands), and *Summa* (Arvo Pärt) replace the *Three Piano Pieces* (Schönberg), *Structures* (Boulez), and *Kadenzen* (Stockhausen) and liberate music from its isolation, couching it with (new) meaning, (new) value. At the same time modern culture is indicted, disregarded, deported to the vaults of history. Affirmation should supplant critical distance; rationality should be substituted by sensuality and emotional appreciation; communication should replace formalistic introspection and experimentation. Music should serve as a kind of contra-ritual to a disenchanted commonplace world.[7] What religion is no longer able to accomplish is now entrusted to the composer. However, one might ask oneself if the qualities of accessibility, familiarity, and clarity (communication) demanded of music, do not equal an attempt to shape music in the image of a technocratic and rationalized world? Perhaps a typical quality of spiritual music is not to give meaning but, on the contrary, to put it in jeopardy through an interruption of meaninglessness.

Spirituality *versus* modernity; ignored, stashed away, is the fact that Stockhausen's alleged spiritual inspirations for composing did not prevent him from developing new musical languages. This is one example. The same goes *mutatis mutandis* for John Cage, Anton Webern and Olivier Messiaen (to restrict myself to just a few musicians from the so-called 'classical' world). Their contributions to Western music are not even pushed aside as 'old spiritual music'; modernistic musical languages simply cannot be spiritual.

The sketched description of a new musical spirituality and its positioning as a movement opposed to other movements converge. They have something in common; the one confirms and consolidates the other like two dance partners. Both do what they have to do by definition, that is, create an ideology of exclusiveness. In the process of establishing a consolidating identity, in order to maintain integrity, and to protect property, a 'strategy of exclusion' seems to be inevitable.

---

[7]   Two short quotes from one of the main guests of the Festival *Nieuwe spirituele muziek*, Dutch composer Joep Franssens, can illustrate this. In an interview he says: "I would define modernism as a position from which reason is overvalued and the emotional appreciation of music is neglected." And continuing with regards to communication: "When my instructors once reproved me for wanting to present the public with a ready-to-eat meal, I thought: Yes, that's right, that's what I want to do" (Franssens 1997: 23).

Almost six years after the Festival, in June 2005, the spectrum of performances and projects in the *Holland Festival* 2005 program is framed by the motto 'Heaven and Hell,' offering a retrospective of *New Spirituality* with the music of Arvo Pärt, John Tavener, and Claude Vivier, to mention only the most well-known. It is striking, although at the same time hardly surprising, that in this festival Heaven is represented by warm, soft, slow, tonal sounds, while the sounds of Hell are harsh, non tonal, and irregular, predominantly produced by classic avant-garde composers such as Iannis Xenakis, Helmut Lachenmann, and John Cage.

What exactly is meant by this strategy of exclusion? One could describe it as a form of negation in which identity is secured by eliminating difference or alterity. It is a struggle for mastery in which an entity asserts itself by reacting against 'the other,' thereby enclosing itself within the secure "solitude of solidity and self-identity" (Derrida 1978: 91). Everything is what it is, the outside is out and the inside in. After all, that is how identity could be defined: the condition or fact that a thing is itself and not something else. Having an identity means being identical-to-oneself by excluding from oneself everything other (than oneself).[8] Identity is that which is different from difference.

The elaborate strategies of self-assertion are actually various efforts to secure self-presence by excluding the dangerous other: both by defining new spiritual music and by depicting it as a movement, 'the other' – being here rather problematic because of the heterogeneous term 'modern music' – is banned to the outside, to the margin, presented as an enemy and an evil. The other is subordinated as well. An identity, a movement, defines itself not only by setting itself in opposition to but also by transcending other isolated identities. At stake is 'an economy of ownership' in which an identity or a self seeks security "by struggling against dispossession, impropriety, and expropriation" (M. Taylor 1984: 131). To be is to be different. This difference marks any identity.[9]

---

[8]   In the previous Threshold I mentioned the *shofars*, ram's horns, with which the Jewish people conquered Jericho. According to tradition these *shofars* were bequeathed to the Jews by Abraham. Genesis 22 tells how Abraham shows himself willing to carry out God's commandment to sacrifice his son Isaac. At the very last moment, God intervenes, dictating Abraham to substitute a ram for Isaac. Abraham offers up the ram but the animal's horns won't burn. He rescues them and donates them to the Jewish people as the central instrument of ritual. Thus it sonically represents Jewish identity (Bohlman 2002: 10).

[9]   Of course, the question is if the movement New Spiritual Music can retain and control its proclaimed homogeneous identity. The movement seems sizeable indeed. The list of names mentioned above is far from complete; important composers often connected to this new spirituality such as John Tavener (UK) and Henryk Gorecki (Poland) should be mentioned. 'Neo-medieval' projects of the American Kronos Quartet and the British Hilliard Ensemble (for example in collaboration with Norwegian saxophone player Jan Garbarek) could also be included. And let's not forget 'popular' subgenres like Celtic spiritual music, New Age music, and CDs with sounds from nature (whales, rainforests, deserts, and so on), which can be listened to in such National Public Radio programs as *Sound and Spirit*. And what about contemporary Gospel music and other (neo-)religious compositions? What about the religious periods of Bob Dylan, Carlos Santana, and Cat Stevens? What about Prince? John McLaughlin, Abdullah Ibrahim (Dollar Brand) and so many other jazz musicians? The movement looks as heterogeneous as its size and its borders are not easily determinable. This heterogeneity also marks the World Festival of Sacred Music in Los Angeles where Mozart's *Requiem* is programmed next to Buddhist chants from the Zangdokpalri monks and nuns, and the sacred musical traditions of Judaism and Sufism sound together with the experimental music of Meredith Monk and the later (sacred) compositions of Duke Ellington.

It is neither the 'newness' nor the 'music-ness' which can be regarded as the prime mover of this strategy of exclusion. The 'music-ness' of both the new spiritual music and modern music guarantees a certain inclusion, a similarity that neutralizes difference. The adjective 'newness' does indeed create an outside. However, in this case, this outside is also an inside, namely an other, older, spiritual music. The actual negation of otherness is here fully on account of the third term: spirituality. Instead of 'new,' one could also use the characterization of 'orthodox,' as this defined movement represses heterodoxy. 'Hetero' meaning 'other' or 'different' in Greek, heterodoxy can (in this sense) be considered as the unacceptable deviation of the *doxa*, of opinion. Orthodoxy ('ortho' meaning straight, right, correct, and proper) represents the effort to master otherness and to control difference (M. Taylor 1984: 88).[10]

This musical spirituality is post-modern in the most literal and hackneyed sense of the word: it succeeds modernistic attainments of and in music and is vehemently opposed to them. Let us return once more to the program notes:

> If only because of the very essential change in the aesthetic and cultural-philosophical foundations of the New Spiritual Music with respect to the traditional avant-garde since World War II, the aggravated attention that the composers of spiritual music will receive during this large-scale festival is justified. In the Western culture of the 1990s, the philosophy of rational modernism has definitely relinquished its dominant position to the more intuitive philosophy of postmodernism.

Spirituality and postmodernism act here on the same plane, beyond and against modernism (although the question could be raised to which extent the qualification of this music as *new* spirituality, in rejection of much of its twentieth-century past, is in fact a modernist trait). New spirituality is presented as an inextricable part of contemporary postmodernism, New Spiritual Music as a movement within the broader concept of postmodern music.

However, that which is often manifested with the more concealing than illuminating term postmodern,[11] cannot this attitude or condition exactly be

---

[10] "Chief opponents of the orthodox are those who err," Taylor writes. He emphasizes the orthodox attempt to establish firm rules that will prevent further erring (M. Taylor 1984: 88). In Threshold 8 I will present my argument that spirituality could exactly be situated in this erring. A possible implication of this suggestion is also to reconsider the term 'movement.' Instead of regarding a movement as a discrete entity, as an inside with clear-cut boundaries, possessing an identity marked by difference, I propose to take the term more literally: as a displacement which by definition indicates an irreducible alterity (Derrida 1981a: 40).

[11] It is far from my aim here to start a feeble effort to define, redefine or undefine this problematic term 'postmodernism.' Many different authors – advocates and opponents – have, in numerous other contexts, rejected the term for its often unworkable vagueness. Postmodernism has become a *passe-partout* concept, still at hand to be applied to all kinds of situations and connections. When everything can potentially be called postmodern, the concept loses its meaning and becomes an empty, indifferent label for no-matter-what.

thought of as a *postexclusivism*?[12] In *Kopernikanische Mobilmachung und ptolemäische Abrüstung* [Copernican Mobilization and Ptolemaic Disarmament], German philosopher Peter Sloterdijk regards postmodernism as a reflective attitude critically questioning the exclusivating tendencies of the modern project. "Principally, postmodernism means nothing but postexclusivism," Sloterdijk writes (Sloterdijk 1987: 49, my translation).[13] In a Heideggerian move, Sloterdijk sketches a postmodern theory that develops no superior discourse or grand narrative but a resigned attentiveness and openness, yet without falling back into a premodern *naïveté*. Precisely this postexclusivism does not carve out a space for postmodernism *after* or *opposite to* modernism. Wolfgang Welsch's book *Unsere postmoderne Moderne* [Our Postmodern Moderns], akin to Jean-François Lyotard's *Le Postmoderne expliqué aux enfants* [*The Postmodern Explained*], clearly testifies to this idea. However different in their approaches, both thinkers situate the postmodern *within* the project of modernity. Put differently, from the outset, the postmodern seems enclosed in the modern project, identity permeated with alterity, 'the other' being part of 'the self.'[14] The prefix *post* only marks a reaction against what Welsch calls 'Die neue Zeit,' the new age, characterized and dominated by identity and unity discourses which always threaten to become totalitarian. So the postmodern condition should

---

However, speaking about postmodernism simultaneously invokes modernism. Like Siamese twins, these two concepts are intertwined. German philosopher Wolfgang Welsch correctly notes in his book *Unsere postmoderne Moderne* that the vagueness of the term postmodernism often reflects the existing obscurity with regard to the term modernism. Many modernisms create just as many postmodernisms. In other words, Charles Chaplin's *Modern Times* does not equal Jean-Paul Sartre's *Les Temps Modernes*. Using the term (post)modernism strongly depends on the discourse within which the use of the term is situated. Within art history, for example, the concept (post)modernity is articulated, used, and phrased quite differently than in the fields of historiography or sociology. This problem of defining both modernism and postmodernism already shows that a subject is not a simple substance or a stable substrate. Rather, a subject, *any* subject, is a complex matrix of ever-changing relations situated in the midst of an extensively and intensively differentiated milieu.

So, no exhaustive description, definition, or explanation of postmodernism will be attempted; however, this does not mean that it is impossible to track down some general orientation or direction so-called 'postmodern thinkers' are advocating. It is their (particular) trace that I am following here.

   [12]   With the term 'attitude,' I am referring to Foucault's interpretation of modernity; 'condition' refers to Lyotard's well-known book *La condition postmoderne* [*The Postmodern Condition*]. Both thinkers consider modernity and postmodernity as a way of thinking and feeling; a way too, of acting and behaving.

   [13]   Postexclusivism should not be mistaken for the slogan 'anything goes.' Canceling out a certain taboo is to be seen as a differentiation of the exclusivating principle, not as an acquiescent pluralism.

   [14]   Trying to formulate an answer to the question "What is Postmodernism?" Lyotard begins with: "It is undoubtedly part of the modern" (Lyotard 1993: 79).

not be considered chronologically as the era *after* modernity (Welsch 1988: 6). A postmodern attitude takes leave of thinking in universalities, unity, and the pathos of exclusion, as far as this leads to uniformization and the overlooking of differences. However, this attitude was always already lurking in the modern project. Exactly through a (modern) orientation on transitions and the flawing of discrete structures, the (postmodern) idea of plurality and particularity finally becomes dominant. The postmodern attitude thus corresponds with a twentieth-century scientific and artistic modernism (Welsch 1988: 36).

The radical nature of these statements should not be omitted. Sloterdijk's notion of postexclusivism resounds in Welsch' suggestion to connect postmodernism with *paralogy*, described by him as the attention for the 'unfamiliar' or the 'uncanny' (Welsch 1988: 34).[15] The following statement by Lyotard can also be understood in this line of thought: "All that has been received, if only yesterday (modo, modo Petronius used to say), must be suspected ... A work can only become modern if it is first postmodern" (Lyotard 1993: 79). According to Lyotard, the postmodern artist creates a work that is not, in principle, governed by pre-established rules and cannot be judged according to a determinant judgment, by the application of given categories to the work. Such rules and categories are, in fact, what the work is investigating. Therefore, the artist works without rules and in order to establish the rules for what will have been made. Art is postmodern so long as it does not discover and obey its rules. Postmodernism is that instance of instability 'prior' to the concretization of rules, 'before' art is joined to a grand narrative (V. Taylor 1999: 16–17).[16] "Postmodernism thus understood is not modernism at its end but in the nascent state, and this state is constant," writes Lyotard (Lyotard 1993: 79).

Where does this rather long digression on (post)modernism bring me? To connect spirituality to postmodernism, to present a new spiritual music as part of a much broader transformation and cultural orientation roughly summarized under the name postmodernism, implies at least recognizing dimensions in cultural fields (music) that question and even transgress prior thinking as regards exclusivity, identity, clear-cut boundaries, and transparency.

---

[15] In *The Postmodern Condition* (1984) Lyotard uses the term in much the same way. According to him paralogy implies an 'irreverent' attitude towards well-accepted theories, breaking them up and recombining them in radically new ways. The point of paralogy is to help us shake ourselves loose of stultifying traditional frameworks which we have come to take for granted in order to enhance our spontaneous creativity.

[16] Taylor's notion of postmodernity seems to me to bear traces of Kant's reflective judgment. The faculty of judgment *in general* allows one to think the particular as contained under the general (rule, principle, law). The *reflective* judgment, on the other hand, has only the particular at its disposal; it is not lead by rules to assess an object. The example is given prior to a law and, through its very uniqueness as example, allows one to discover that particular law afterwards.

Reestablishing the triangle music–spirituality–postmodernism thus creates an alternative space, a space where thinking in binary oppositions can be deconstructed, a space where identity can no longer be separated from difference and alterity, a space where musical spirituality can no longer withdraw into a safe, familiar, and reassuring reclining-upon accessibility and unproblematized self-presence. The presented interrelationship of modernism and postmodernism not only inverts but subverts the exclusive logic of identity. Otherness and relations to other(s) are intrinsic to and necessary for any determination whatsoever.

It is precisely this loss of identity, this interruption of the logic of exclusion, and this total reciprocity that I would like to connect with a (post)modern notion of spirituality. Therefore, I should first leave behind me the idea that spiritual music is a movement which can be regarded as being opposed to modern music. Perhaps I should even say farewell to the idea that something which can be named spiritual music exists.[17]

With this first and cautious rethinking of spirituality and its possible relation to music, I do not want to oppose myself to the various liberation movements organized in the name of spirituality but rather to that in the name of which and ultimately, therefore, for the sake of which they are organized and made practical and concrete: identity itself. That is, I am objecting to the particular 'political' ends to which the possibly non-aligned, non-categorizable spiritual experiences are sometimes subordinated. And to the language surrounding spirituality which colludes in that process of subordination, recuperating the aspiration to being-beyond to being-as.[18] It is my aim to reconsider spirituality *through* music and its surrounding discourse by including and accepting the heterodoxical (and even para-doxical) elements that permeate contemporary (post-modern) thinking. And it is perhaps *through* music that an experience with a spirituality that can never be contained, captured, or caught by any fixed pair of terms,

---

[17]   Interestingly enough, it is precisely one of the alleged mainstays of the New Spiritual Music movement who instigates this way of thinking. In an interview with Emile Wennekes in the Dutch daily *De Volkskrant* (6 November 1999), Giya Kancheli confides to the journalist that he has no clue as to what this new spirituality in music means: "Personally, that is of no use to me. In my opinion, there is no separation between spiritual and non-spiritual music. All good [*sic*] music has spiritual qualities, Webern's and Ligeti's as much as Arvo Pärt's" (my translation).

[18]   These thoughts are (sometimes literally) based on the ideas expressed by Geraldine Finn in her book *Why Althusser Killed His Wife* (1996), especially pp. 152–65. Her remarks on postmodernism and spirituality were a great source of inspiration for my writings and traverse this book as a leitmotiv.

becomes possible.[19] What is a spirituality beyond dual oppositions, and what does the word 'beyond' mean here?

---

[19] In the opening text of *Dissemination*, 'Outwork,' Derrida warns against putting old names to work, or even just leaving them in circulation. The risk is to settle down or to regress back into the system that has been, or is in the process of being, deconstructed. To deny this risk would be to confirm it, Derrida writes. It would be to see the signifier – in this case the name 'spirituality' – as a merely circumstantial, conventional occurrence of the concept. It would be an affirmation of the autonomy of meaning. Inversely, simply to reject previous marks means to forget that (the use of) these marks (marks like 'spirituality') have never constituted a given system, a sort of ahistorical, thoroughly homogeneous table, but rather a space whose closure is constantly being traversed by the forces and (re)worked by the exteriority that it represses: that is, expels and (which amounts to the same) internalizes as one of its moments. In other words, can that which has always been conceived and signified under the name of spirituality be considered fundamentally homogeneous, univocal, or non-conflictual? If we are compelled to answer this question in the negative, could we then maintain the statement that the rethinking of the concept 'spirituality' already breaks away from that other, older, previous spirituality – away from what has already been conceived and signified under that name – or that which, not merely escaping spirituality, implacably destroys it? (Derrida 1981a: 3–5.) In my opinion, spirituality should be thought of as 'something' that escapes language and (thus) has no name. The only way to bring 'it' up, provisionally, is to reuse the names we do have. Perhaps we should call 'spirituality' a *quasi-catachresis*: an improperly used word for 'something' that has no name and which does not, after its designation, evoke any concrete images.

THRESHOLD 5
Between Heaven and Earth

IN the first volume of *À la recherche du temps perdu*, *Du côté de chez Swann*, Marcel Proust narrates the love affair between Charles Swann and Odette. An insufferably hypocritical and obnoxious bourgeois couple, the Verdurins, introduces them to each other at one of their nightly salons. There, the Verdurins repeatedly play a sonata for violin and piano, produced by a fictitious composer, Monsieur Vinteuil. The piercing violin crescendos make Swann so happy that an association in his mind between the music and his burgeoning love for Odette becomes fixed. The sonata has the power to conjure up Swann's feelings for Odette even when he tries not to think of her. As Swann craves to hear Vinteuil's composition, the music becomes the 'theme' for him and Odette. He feels the sonata lifting his spirits and making his love for her seem stronger than anything else in the world. When Swann later learns that Odette's feelings for him constitute only a flirtatious infatuation, he lets the music carry him back to the happy moments when she at least pretended to love him. Swann describes his intense response, especially to a little phrase in the sonata, as if it belonged to

> ... an order of *supernatural* creatures whom we have never seen, but whom, in spite of that, we recognize and acclaim with rapture when some explorer of the unseen contrives to coax it forth, *to bring it down from the divine world* to which he has access to shine for a brief moment in the firmament of ours. (Proust 1954: 363, my italics)

Is Proust writing about spiritual music here? He does not name it as such, but it is very well possible to recognize in this quote something that might be considered a spiritual origin of music. This music seems, in the narration of Proust, to be otherworldly or at least coming from an other world.[1] The important difference

---

[1]   Considering (certain) music as a gift from a transcendent world, is a well-known belief that appears throughout the history of ideas regarding music's origin. I confine myself to three rudimentary examples here.

To Hesiod (eighth–seventh century BC) the nine Muses – equivalent to the Angels of monotheism – appear as messengers who accost human beings such as poets and musicians, charging them with a divine mission. The implication of the Muses' patronage of the arts is that the arts in their essence are no human invention but a gift of superhuman origin and inspiration, reflecting some form of universal wisdom and knowledge (Godwin 1987: 169–70).

In the *Li Chi*, the ancient Chinese Book of Rites whose compilation was begun by Confucius (551–478 BC), music is a reflection of the perfect harmony of the heavens: "Harmony is the thing principally sought in music: – it therein follows Heaven, and manifests the expansive spiritual influence characteristic of it" (*Li Chi*, XVII, I: 29). According to the *Li Chi*, music arouses harmonious effects in the human domain because everybody shares the same emotions when listening collectively to it (Godwin 1987: 40–41).

Ernst Hagemann, reporting and interpreting the music philosophy of the founder of the Anthroposophic Movement, Rudolf Steiner (1861–1925), says that, regarding music, there are archangels, spirits of music, who convey certain powers, senses, and consciousness impulses. Behind all tones that we perceive is spiritual being. Tones therefore exist in a twofold mode: as vibrating air and as an inner experience on the etheric and astral level (Godwin 1987: 159).

between the two lies in the belief that we, human mortals, presumably are not even equipped with the abilities to perceive those heavenly sounds with our confined senses: we need some kind of translation, some kind of transformation in order to be exposed to them. One could say that this music, coming from a transcendental world but made audible for ordinary mortals, is situated *between* heaven and earth: it has to be brought down from the divine world in order to sound in the human vaults of heaven. And it is the composer who acts as some kind of messenger or intermediary between these two worlds.[2] In *Harmonies of Heaven and Earth*, (speculative) music historian Joscelyn Godwin claims that composers are therefore a type of alchemists who help "to transmute the earth by making its substance and souls resonate with echoes of the heavenly music."[3] In doing so, the gap between the two becomes constricted a little bit (Godwin 1987: 81).[4]

---

[2]   Sometimes an extra intermediary is needed as becomes clear in the legend on the origin of Gregorian chant. It is in John the Deacon's biography on Pope St Gregory I (±580–604), written around 872, that we can read how Gregory 'the Great' dictates to a scribe the melodies that a heavenly dove, perched on his shoulder, is whispering into his ears, finally resulting in the *Liber Antiphonarius*, the book containing several thousand liturgical chants.

[3]   Godwin sustains a tradition that Jamie James calls 'the Great Theme' – "the belief that the cosmos is a sublimely harmonious system [Pythagoras calls this *musica mundana* or the music of the spheres, 'music' which cannot be heard by the human ear but that exists in the realm of pure intellect] guided by a Supreme Intelligence, and that man has a place preordained and eternal in that system" (James 1995: 19). In *The Music of the Spheres* (1995), James describes the perpetuation of this thought of 'scientifically proven' cosmic harmony until now, from its Pythagorasian origin where harmony in the soul is patterned after the harmony of the universe, through its decline when science began to reveal certain shortcomings in the theory, cultural theories shifted their emphasis from the cosmic to the human, and divinity was to be found in the spirit of man (the Romantic genius and virtuoso), not in a remote cosmos, to the revival of 'the Great Theme' in the music of Arnold Schönberg (his rationally constructed *Gurrelieder* as well as his more mystical pieces *Die Jakobsleiter* and *Moses und Aaron* put him in the Pythagorean tradition) and Karl-Heinz Stockhausen (in the cycle of seven operas called *Licht* Stockhausen closely follows Boethius's division of music into the congruent realms of *musica mundana*, *musica humana*, and *musica instrumentalis*).

[4]   Sounds that seem properly at home in an intermediate etheric world between earth and heaven have their counterpart in music that joins earth and hell. Hell also has a musical realm and the devil himself is known to be a staggeringly good fiddler. However, the devil's musical skills serve one purpose only: the seduction of souls. He inverts the purpose of god-given harmony, using the power to drag the soul not up but down. Meaningful in this respect is the *Diabolus in musica* ('the devil in music'), a medieval name for the tritone, the diminished fifth, so called because of its extremely dissonant sound. Another case in point is Giuseppe Tartini's (1692–1770) sonata *Il trillo del diavolo* (The Devil's Trill Sonata). One night in 1713, while fast asleep, Tartini dreamt that the devil stood at the foot of his bed, trying to bargain for his soul. Whatever Tartini wanted was granted to him, and all his wishes were anticipated by his new servant. The devil also gave him a violin to see if he could play anything harmonious. Tartini challenged the devil to a musical duel. To his astonishment, the devil played with consummate skill a sonata of exquisite beauty. When he

Staying within the Hermetic tradition – Hermes, son of Zeus, supreme ruler of the Pantheon of gods, and the nymph Maia, is the herald, the swift messenger of the Olympian gods, constantly traveling between heaven and earth – Godwin speculates about the state of these artists: are they superhuman beings who have descended to earth, or are they men who in the course of long striving have managed to enter the portals of heaven? (Godwin 1987: 85.)[5]

Although only a few composers have (had) the privilege to conceive the progeny of the gods, many of them, especially those living and working in the Romantic era, claim to be transmitters of spiritual music: Wagner, Brahms, Puccini, Grieg, and Strauss are but a few who talk about their music as coming through and to them from another, higher world.[6] They are no longer creators of a music whose 'musicness' actually lies *behind* the phenomenal object of a work; they are intermediaries through which the spiritual achieves an empirical form.

The testimonies of these composers resonate in Rudolf Steiner's words regarding the relationship between artistic creativity and the state of consciousness encountered while asleep, provided that a sufficient degree of spiritual initiation has already been attained. Steiner first distinguishes between the astral world, a glorious play of light and color, and the angelic or Devachanic world (*deva* means 'angel' or 'demigod' in Sanskrit), a world of tones, both of which can be experienced while sleeping. The initiate enters these worlds consciously, whereas the vast majority remains unaware of where they have been. Steiner, however, recognizes another stage, intermediate between these two, which is the experience of the inspired, creative artist: he may not remember consciously where he has been, but still he is able to reproduce something of what he saw or heard there.

---

awoke, Tartini attempted to reproduce the netherworldy music of his dream, and as a result wrote his most famous G minor sonata.

5   In *World Music*, Philip Bohlman writes:

Just as myths tell about the intersections between the natural and the supernatural, or between humans and deities, so too they tell about how music emerges at the points of intersection ... Music realizes the ways in which individuals cohabit these several worlds, allowing the worshipper to perform these worlds simultaneously. (Bohlman 2002: 2 and 14)

6   "I have very definite impressions while in that trance-like condition, which is the prerequisite of all true creative effort. I feel that I am one with this vibrating Force, that it is omniscient, and that I can draw upon it to an extent that is limited only by my own capacity to do so," Wagner told his friend and colleague Engelbert Humperdinck (Abell 1994: 138).

The utterances of Karl-Heinz Stockhausen, speaking of his own origins on the star Sirius, can be considered a more contemporary continuation of this tradition. According to him, we can bring ourselves through music into relationship with that which we cannot grasp with the understanding, with the Supernatural, with God, with the Spirit who holds everything together.

"The melodies and harmonies that speak to us from the works of our great masters are faithful copies of the Devachanic world. If we can obtain a shadow, a foretaste of the Devachanic world in anything, it is in the effects of the melodies and harmonies of music, in their effects on the human soul … Man's original home is in Devachan, and the echoes from this homeland, this spiritual world, resound in him in the harmonies and melodies of the physical world. These echoes pervade our world with the presentiments of a glorious and wonderful existence; they throng through his innermost being and thrill it with vibrations of purest joy, of sublimest spirituality, which this lower world cannot provide," Steiner writes (quoted in Godwin 1987: 81–2).

So the 'chosen' or 'inspired' composers – themselves in a double inbetweenness as they are suspended on a putatively existential level situated between heaven and earth while at the same time existing on the level of consciousness somewhere between the initiates and the laypersons – introduce us to an inbetweenness of music evoking divine feelings using human means.[7] Music, spiritual music, is both heavenly and earthly. I could refer here as well to an infrequently used meaning of the word 'spirit' as 'the one who kidnaps' or 'an abductor.' The spiritual dimension of music draws the two clearly located opposites away from their 'natural' position.

The notion of spiritual music as an intermediate state constantly reappears in Godwin's book. Retaining the Latin meaning of the word *spiritus* as neither body nor soul (later Godwin replaces the latter by 'mind') but something that in some way unites them, Godwin draws from the book *De vita coelitus comparanda* [On Fitting One's Life to the Heavens], written by the Renaissance Platonist, philosopher, and priest Marsilio Ficino (1433–99). According to Ficino, one of the best ways of improving the spirit is through music. This is because the medium of sound, air, is the most similar to it in substance.[8] He describes part of music's operations as follows: musical sound by the movement of the air moves the body. By purified air it excites the aerial *spiritus* which is the bond of body and soul; by emotion it affects the senses and at the same time the soul.[9] *De vita* offers a set of practical techniques for creating songs that will draw down beneficial planetary

---

[7] "Musicians […] populate many mythological and religio-philosophical writings about the origins of religion and history. These […] musicians occupy the transitional spaces between what is not human and what is … We witness these […] musicians precisely at those mythological moments when identity is most critically called into question, particularly the identities that distinguish sacred realms from secular" (Bohlman 2002: 9–10).

[8] One of the meanings of the Latin word *spiritus* is 'breathing,' 'breath,' or 'air.' According to Ficino, sound affects the spirits more strongly than sight because it transmits movement and is itself moving, whereas vision is concerned with static images. Because man's whole moral and emotional life consists of actions of the body and motions of the spirit and soul, these can be imitated in music and transmitted by it (Gouk 2004: 103).

[9] Ficino, Marsilio, *Three Books on Life* (New York: MRTS, 1989). See especially book 3, chapter XXI.

emanations to restore the spirits. As such, musical sound serves as the link between heavenly and earthly domains. The nexus between natural and human spirits is thus 'automatic' in the sense that it bypasses the will and is confined to the sensory level and imagination (Gouk 2004: 102).

The spirit, regarded by Ficino as a corporeal vapor flying through the blood to the brain, serves and connects body and the incorporeal soul/mind without being convertible into one of them. A third element and milieu crosses the abyss of those two absolutely heterogeneous wor(l)ds. *Spiritus* must be treated as a separable part but also as a nondetachable part, since it forms the articulation between the other two. And this intermediate domain of the spirit is also the place where music is inscribed.

Thinking along the same lines as Ficino, more than five centuries later and from a phenomenological standpoint, one could say that music takes (its) place between the etherical and the corporeal. The world in which music exists is a spiritual world. Music is an art in time, flowing in a bodiless world. It surpasses the borders of the universe of bodies. We cannot grasp music in the same way that we can touch and feel matter in our world. Like air, music does not show itself. But even when we thus assume a close connection between music and spirit, this spiritual dimension needs to be incarnated in order to sound, which means that this incarnation is no accidental supplement, but an inevitable necessity. Not only do we need our ears to hear music, the musician needs his body and/as an instrument to awaken music. Ears, drumming hands, stamping feet, the bow that moves the strings of the cello: these are all part of a bodily world. Music is born in a space that connects a spiritual and an embodied world.[10]

Not directly translatable or understandable as music's inbetweenness though very much related to it, Godwin points out that in some Oriental philosophies, music deconstructs the binary opposition between subject and object. The experience of music entails both an objective material world as well as a subjective one. In the objective world, instruments are played, and air and eardrums vibrate. The subjective world consists of musical emotions, images, and rational thoughts. But, as Godwin explains, the subjective world is no more the result of the objective one than its cause: the two "simply arise together as twin aspects of a single event" (Godwin 1987: 28–9). In the course of contemplating an object – music, for example – a subject may dissolve into the sounds heard and for a while become identified with it, so that the music is experienced as indistinguishable from the subject.[11]

---

[10] I thank Dutch philosopher Ruud Welten who lead my thoughts in this direction.

[11] Though Godwin particularly mentions the Sufi tradition, within the Western philosophical tradition someone like Georges Bataille articulates more or less the same idea. Bataille calls the familiar and rational world in which we live 'homogeneous' and 'discontinuous.' In this world, beings are presented as delimited, autonomous and therefore discontinuous unities. However, the universe according to Bataille is nothing but movement, the world a wild field of flowing energy and excessive flux, continuous, one immense plain

This line of thought is not confined to Oriental philosophy. American composer and music theorist John Rahn writes, "human life and music listened to by that life do not run parallel in straight lines never meeting, but rather intertwine closely, touching each other all over, each penetrating and being penetrated by the other, so that while they touch they almost fuse into one entity, one life-music or one music-life" (Harvey 1999: 30). The experience of music, Rahn states, affords a person to set himself free from the polar opposition subject–object.[12] "Music is intimately concerned with transcending that dichotomy" is one of Jonathan Harvey's first sentences when he starts exploring the relation between music and spirituality in his book *In Quest of Spirit* (1999).

Though Oriental philosophies as well as Rahn, Godwin, and Harvey construe this 'deconstruction' of the subject–object opposition, that is, its fundamental closure, as a step towards (spiritual) wholeness and unity, a convergence of differences that celebrates the principle of sameness in order to avoid the dehiscing effects of difference,[13] I think it paves the way for thinking the interbeing, the in-between once more. Not even clearly localizable between the two quantities, no longer determined as an equal power between one of the fundamental oppositions of modern Western thought, this inbetweenness designates a transversal movement that effaces one and the other. The blurring of the opposed identities is not sublated but constantly permeates and haunts binary thinking.[14]

---

of heterogeneous energy. What Bataille defines as the sacred or the spiritual, a thought in which I follow him to a great extent, is transgression, a submission to the discontinuity of the world in which the boundaries of an 'I' are floating.

A central theme in his thinking is the 'inner experience,' an experience in which both subject and object lose their familiar contours and appear as radical indeterminacies. Deviating from Godwin and the Sufi tradition, Bataille states that the object is experienced as an unknown, and the subject experiences himself as not-knowing and heterogeneous. This experience cannot depend on any external criterion or any center 'hors-texte.' It is an experience – Bataille calls it 'sovereign' – of the loss of every stable sense.

[12]   Many other examples could be quoted here. Karl-Heinz Stockhausen, for example, argues that in concentrating to the greatest possible degree on sounds themselves, one is completely swallowed up; one *becomes* music.

[13]   Jonathan Harvey, referring to Zen Buddhist koans (formulas, questions, exercises conveying an appearance of rationality which can only be solved through meditation) speaks of this 'unity in ambiguity' as an enlightened understanding (Harvey 1999: 33). The persuasion that the complete reality forms a spiritual-material unity in which all phenomena are connected through a process of becoming can also be found in the Western alchemistic traditions. In *The Magic Flute: An Alchemical Allegory* (Leiden: Brill, 2004), Dutch theologian Tjeu van den Berk interprets Mozart's last opera completely from this perspective.

[14]   According to Mircea Eliade, an experience of the spiritual, a hierophany, is a transfiguration of an order. A hierophantic moment is one in which two experiences are held contradictorily, equally, and simultaneously. These two distinct experiences do not form a dialectic or generate a sublation, but rather mark a fissure in the surface and depth of knowledge. The fabric of knowledge is thus interrupted by an experience of the spiritual.

Neither merging nor conventional communication between autonomous beings: what remains after the loss of distinction is a gaping breach where neither 'alone' nor 'together' can exist any longer.[15]

Neither subject nor object. Connecting body and soul. Between heaven and earth. Determining an unambiguous place for the spirituality of music seems a complex task.[16] Maybe we could even assume from these examples – perhaps prematurely, but to some extent, and certainly with utmost reticence, in agreement with Godwin and Rahn's texts – that music's spiritual dimension has no clearly definable place of its own, no well-defined *topos*. Its inbetweenness seems to mean 'both … and' and 'neither … nor.' Music's spirituality is heavenly as well as earthly and simultaneously none of these two, that is, it cannot be reduced to one of the poles. However, this intermediary state is also not a third place, as in a kind of dialectic move where the opposites are sublated. The oppositions are unsettled; but this is not done by stepping outside the oppositions, by introducing a new space that functions equal to or above the other two. The inbetweenness seems to resist and disorganize the oppositions without ever constituting a third term and without ever leaving room for a dialectical solution. In that sense, the place of this intermediary member is at once deprived of place. Or at least it runs the risk, in taking place, of not achieving its own proper domain (Derrida 1987: 38). This non-localizable place of music's spirituality turns out to be an uninterrupted transference or displacement; it is always suspended – a play between two realms – and this suspension permanently creates a kind of blank or interval.

The observations made so far are not so concerned with the question *what* the spiritual dimension of music might be, as *where* this dimension might be situated, though the paradoxical, disenchanting answer is that it has no place. It seems that the where-question can be answered only if we radically give up thinking in fixed locations or nameable places. With Foucault, we could say that the 'common locus'

In that sense, the spiritual 'transcends' as it were, profane categorizations. It exists in the hollows and folds of (Western) logocentrism (V. Taylor 1999: 63 and 69).

Translated back to the subject–object dichotomy, Mark Taylor writes: "The inscription of the subject within this tissue of relations results in the collapse of the absolute opposition between interiority and exteriority. If the subject is not self-centered but is a cipher for forces that play through it, there can be no sharp opposition between outwardness and inwardness" (M. Taylor 1984: 136).

[15] This idea is expressed very well in the verb 'to be in love with.' The acceding to the love is not connected to a feature or mood of the lovers nor to a relation that presupposes possession; this acceding refers primarily to a site (*in* love) where the lovers devote themselves to a moment of both presence and absence in order to enter completely into a (single, unique) 'in-between.'

[16] In a public lecture in 2003, Jonathan Harvey stated that "between the transition from one to the other, there is a no man's land that belongs to neither of them," a no man's land where "identity is questioned."

has been lost. This is what Foucault calls an *a-topia*, literally a non-place, a white spot on the map of language, the hole in language, the opposite of *topos*, meaning both place and commonplace (Foucault 1971: xviii). More radically, entering the domain of Derrida's deconstructive philosophy, an atopia could be thought of as a state of 'being' which cannot be covered by oppositions; it constitutes a medium in which the opposites are opposed (Derrida 1981a: 127).[17] A medium. A middle. Both belonging to both opposites and not belonging to either one of them. To conceive of this atopia can be a real stumbling block.[18]

But what does it actually mean to have no place? What are the (inevitable) implications of the spiritual dimension of music Godwin and so many others have traced? To have no place (also) means to be unnamable. It (also) means to have no place within the categorical and classification systems of Western thinking.[19] Atopia is the (non)place where Western thought breaks down. Roland Barthes, for example, considers atopia as 'something' that cannot be laid down by or in definitions or qualifications. In *Roland Barthes by Roland Barthes*, he imagines atopia as a kind of refuge, exempt from fixating denominators (Barthes 1991: 53).[20] But the thinker who most profoundly thematizes the non-space of spirituality, spirituality as an encounter with the inhuman, with what falls outside of every order, a radical otherness that also deconstructs and transects the opposition Self–Other, is indubitably Georges Bataille. His 'God' is no longer the God of the large and institutionalized religions, his 'theology' no longer their theology. Enthralled by mystic traditions, Bataille proposes an *a*-theology, the impossibility to speak about God or man's impossibility to become reconciled with God through communion. What appeals to Bataille is a

---

[17] "That which indicates itself as mysticism, in order to shake the security of discursive knowledge, refers beyond the opposition of the mystic and the rational," Derrida writes in *Writing and Difference* (Derrida 1978: 272). Mysticism – relying on Michel de Certeau, I allow myself to replace this word by its nonsubstitutable synonym 'spirituality' – deconstructs any binary opposition, even the one which opposes spirituality to (one of) its opposites.

[18] Stumbling block is another meaning of the word 'threshold.'

[19] According to Pierre Hadot, by the time of the Platonic dialogues, Socrates was called atopia, that is, 'unclassifiable.' The fact that he is a philosopher, literally the lover of wisdom, makes him atopia. Wisdom is not a human state; knowledge can only be divine. Therefore, the love of wisdom is foreign to the world, making the philosopher a stranger in it.

[20] According to Barthes, the atopia is preferable to the utopia, because the latter is merely a form of reaction, a counterpart or contrast to already existing forms. For Foucault utopias afford consolation: "Although they have no real locality, there is nevertheless a fantastic, untroubled region in which they are able to unfold ... They run with the very grain of language and are part of the fundamental dimension of the *fabula*," he writes in his preface to *The Order of Things* (Foucault 1971: xviii). And Gianni Vattimo describes the objective to unite the aesthetic and the existential or the ordinary as the main utopia of the late twentieth century. In more general terms, utopia refers to the framing of a universal history in one single development. Like Foucault, Vattimo opposes this idea of utopia with heterotopia, a staggering plurality of models, a plurality that can even be applied as a normative criterion against the dominance of one ideal (Vattimo 1998: 81–93).

mysticism that leaves the spiritual unnamed. Bataille's spirituality recognizes and affirms the empty place, left behind after 'the death of God';[21] affirming, that is, not filling the gap again by creating, for example, a new entity, a new quantity, a new center. When in spite of this, Bataille still holds on to the concept 'God,' he writes that it is without form and without mode, a presence that is no longer in any way distinct from an absence, an obstacle in a movement that brings us to a more obscure conception of the unknown. The death of God, regarded as the ultimate sacrifice of modern culture, is an endeavor to retrieve a spiritual dimension at the expense of Reason. An endeavor, because Bataille is aware of the difficulties of avoiding the enclosure of the unknown in some form of knowledge once again.[22] The conversion from a non-place into a *topos* and the absorption of the in-between into well-defined categories are processes constantly lurking.

---

[21] In aphorism 125 in *The Gay Science*, Nietzsche proclaims God's death:

Have you not heard of that madman who lit a lantern in the bright morning hours, ran to the market place, and cried incessantly: "I seek God! I seek God!" – As many of those who did not believe in God were standing around just then, he provoked much laughter. Has he got lost? asked one. Did he lose his way like a child? asked another. Or is he hiding? Is he afraid of us? Has he gone on a voyage? Emigrated? – Thus they yelled and laughed. "Whither is God?" he cried. "I will tell you. *We have killed him*—you and I! All of us are his murderers! But how did we do this? How could we drink up the sea? Who gave us the sponge to wipe away the entire horizon? What were we doing when we unchained this earth from its sun? Whither is it moving now? Whither are we moving? Away from all suns? Are we not plunging continually? And backward, sideward, forward, in all directions? Is there still any up or down? Are we not straying as through an infinite nothing? Do we not feel the breath of empty space? Has it not become colder? Is not night continually closing in on us? Do we not need to light lanterns in the morning? Do we not hear nothing as yet of the noise of the gravediggers who are burying God? Do we smell nothing as yet of the divine decomposition? – Gods, too, decompose! God is dead! God remains dead! And we have killed him!

[22] It should also be emphasized that Bataille is not completely rejecting and ignoring Reason. Like prohibition and order, Reason is necessary to survive; however, says Bataille, so is their infringement. A society not based on Reason and order would immediately disintegrate, could not even come into being. Besides, prohibition and the need for order is an inextricable part of our existence. Criticizing Reason, however, is necessary to prevent the confinement of absolutism or totalitarianism. Every structure, every regulation excludes 'otherness'; attention should be drawn to this, on a social as well as an individual level. Bataille asks us to recognize and accept a certain disorder and uncertainty, to open a space where meaninglessness can be experienced. Humans who are able to free themselves from the belief in a stable center of existence, from the belief in teleological and essentialist thoughts, humans who are open to the utmost ambivalent experience of 'otherness' are called sovereign by Bataille. 'Sovereign,' however, in no way equals 'superior.' No higher form of knowledge can be expected; sovereignty on the contrary opens the way towards a total elusiveness.

Bataille is not writing on music. Instead, he turns to poetry, interpreted as the sacrifice of words, as an undermining of the authority of words and sentences, thereby leading both writer and reader into a realm of insecurity, from the known to the unknown. Poetry is for Bataille the endurable form of the ultimate sacrifice made by the death of God.[23] Of course, soon after the enunciation of the poetic words, the familiar images present themselves; however, "they are solicited only in order to die" (Bataille 1998: 135). It is here that Bataille recognizes poetry's inbetweenness. Its sacrifice can be situated between 'the realm of project,' where familiarity and security is guaranteed, and the mere transgression of this project, opening a position where any possibility for identification fails, an atopia.[24]

While elaborating his thoughts on poetry, it is remarkable that Bataille focuses his attention on Proust's *À la recherche du temps perdu*. Why? More than by poetry itself, which develops too often into a practice, a craft, a profession, thereby subjugating the words to a project, Bataille is fascinated by the coincidental, non-preconceived poetic character of an (arbitrary) text. At the end of his excursion on Proust, he criticizes poetry, understood as capacity, accomplishment, aptitude. He is looking for another poetry:

> Poetic genius is not verbal talent (verbal talent is necessary, since it is a question of words, but it often leads one astray): it is the divining of ruins secretly expected, in order that so many immutable things become undone, lose themselves, communicate. Nothing is rarer. This instinct which divines and the act even definitely requires, of one who is in possession of it, silence, solitude: and the more it inspires, all the more cruelly it isolates. (Bataille 1988: 149)

Bataille is thus not dealing with poetry as genre; language is poetical if it offers a shimmer of 'otherness' for a moment. Poetry is another name for a certain discursive disturbance. This disturbance is possible within every genre.

Would it be possible, thinkable, that music meets Bataille's appeal to poetry to lead us from the known to the unknown, from certainty to uncertainty, from a topological notion of spirituality to an a-topological notion? And if we could answer this question in the affirmative, is this a power of all music or must we exclude certain musics?[25] Does something like 'non-spiritual music' exist and is

---

[23]   As such, it is also an inadequate sacrifice. However, every sacrifice is in effect inadequate, that is, permeated with an ambiguity: after all, a sacrifice implies outliving death and forms thereby the actual negation of a real sacrifice.

[24]   Bataille describes this (non)position as the immorality of poetry (Bataille 1988: 137).

[25]   One of the main questions throughout this book will be whether the musico-spiritual is a specific quality, an intrinsic characteristic of a particular kind of music, or if the connection between spirituality and music is established through a relation between music and listener. The first option legitimizes a movement like New Spiritual Music, whereas the second could lead to the conclusion that all music 'contains,' in principle, the spiritual. A group of Orthodox Jews, called Lubavitchers, adhere to this latter opinion. Unlike text, music is for them connected to the spiritual or divine. However, their music, consisting of

this music already excluded by the movement adorned with the name 'spiritual music'? And *where* could this music be that has no place of its own? Big questions. Many questions. They are directing the way, my way of thinking, a way discovered after (de)positioning spirituality – through music as well as in music – as a space between.

The next threshold will resume these reflections in order to elaborate on music that has no place of its own, music that is out-of-place.

---

paraliturgical melodies, is frequently borrowed from the mundane music of the host culture. According to the Lubavitchers, this borrowed music needs their intervention to be freed from its mundane setting. It is considered to be raw but to contain trapped properties of *simhah* (joy) and *hitlahavut* (enthusiasm): two essential emotional states needed in order to live one's life with the proper godly intention (*kavannah*), and therefore to be worthy of adoption and adaptation by Lubavitchers. Performing their music readies them for divine communication, enabling them to communicate with God (cf. Koskoff 1993). Contrary to Bataille's thinking, and contrary also to the ideas on spirituality I am presenting here, Lubavitchers regard their spiritual quest as a journey towards 'oneness' or unity with the divine (*devekuth*). This quest, then, is regarded as a movement away from disorder toward order. Throughout this book I will explain why I think that a connection between spirituality and 'unity,' 'the divine,' and 'order' can be subject to reconsideration or supplementation.

THRESHOLD 6
Sirens

W HERE do I arrive in the process of tracing an a-topological music in the Western history of civilization? Which musical lead might I find in the roots of Western cultural history that could take me to a criticism of logocentrism, a (non)site on which the enduring waves of classification and categorization fall to pieces thereby opening a space to encounter 'something' that could be called spiritual? And how would such a musical lead sound?

Perhaps I should resort to an isle – this aporetic place without guaranteed entrance or exit, without a borderland, without predictable map or calculable program – an isle from which – so the story goes – only a few men have ever returned alive. One of them received warnings in advance so that he could take his precautions. He was cautioned about these islanders, fabulous monsters, part woman, part bird, who were luring sailors to destruction. A sorceress named Circe acted as his siren. But we, who have banished and exterminated our witches or at least ignored them, how will we be warned about imminent violence or immediate peril? By an audible signal perhaps, penetrating and resonant? By a technological device inflicting an acoustic force that demands immediate attention or action? Or is it simply unnecessary, in our current situation, that we be alerted? Let us assume, at least for the time being, that we can and should approach mythical legends as topical realities. Let us consider, albeit with a certain reticence, mythical figures as symbolic identities, who, on the level of myth, can be experienced as projections of our own (im)possibilities.[1] In that case, a warning is still called for, a siren necessary.[2]

So, what exactly is it that Odysseus should be afraid of? Against which lethal weapon must he protect himself? How shocking the answer: music! The singing of the Sirens is enchanting but deadly:

---

[1]   In *Was heißt Denken?* [*What is Called Thinking?*] Heidegger writes that 'mythos' just like 'logos' refers to telling, that is, to lay bare and make appear (Heidegger 1968: 10). The telling or depicting of myths means the making present of creative forces: by returning to ancient times, the existing and the given are disposed of their casualness. Myths can be regarded as dramatizations used in search of a relation towards the inscrutable.

In *La società trasparente* [*The Transparent Society*], Gianni Vattimo regards a myth not as a primitive phase that is defeated by our cultural history, but as a more authentic form of knowledge, unperturbed by the devastating fanaticism for quantification and objectification, typical of modern science, technology, and capitalism. Though not radically opposed to scientific knowledge (described by Vattimo as just another myth), a myth's nature is not proving or analytical, but narrative and imaginative (Vattimo 1998: 46–9).

In *On Stories*, Richard Kearney writes: "The synchronizing power of mythic narrative is often contrasted with the 'hot' historicity of Enlightenment progress. But things are not so simple. In the national narratives of many modern nations, for example, both forms of temporality – hot and cold, progressive and mythic – overlap to form a strangely ambivalent experience" (Kearney 2002: 88).

[2]   Regarded this way, Steely Dan's lyrics "The danger on the rocks is surely past" in 'Home at Last' sound a bit too optimistic. Myths make clear that the past is never totally past (Kearney 2002: 88).

> And that man who unsuspecting approaches them, and listens to the Sirens singing, has no prospect of coming home and delighting his wife and little children as they stand about him in greeting, but the Sirens by the melody of their singing enchant him.

This is the advance warning of the Sirens' danger which Odysseus receives from Circe. Their song, their 'melody of singing' seems to mesmerize, to entrance, and to assert a magnetic force upon those who chance to encounter it. For those men, every hope for a safe return evaporates as they waste away on the beach of the Sirens "piled with boneheaps of men now rotted away." The sorceress, however, continues by giving Odysseus specific instructions as to how he can pass by the songstresses unharmed:

> You must drive straight on past, but melt down sweet wax of honey and with it stop your companions' ears, so none can listen; the rest, that is, but if you yourself are wanting to hear them, then have them tie you hand and foot on the fast ship, standing upright against the mast with the ropes' ends lashed around it, so that you can have joy in hearing the song of the Sirens; but if you supplicate your men and implore them to set you free, then they must tie you fast with even more lashings.

This advice gives Odysseus the possibility to listen to the Sirens' song without physically giving into its spellbinding allure. Though Circe is the actual deviser, the plan is known as Odysseus' trick.

In *Dialektik der Aufklärung* [*Dialectic of Enlightenment*] Max Horkheimer and Theodor Adorno read this trick as one of the first acts of Reason in Western cultural history.[3] It is an attempt to exorcize the power of music, to subject it hierarchically to instrumental reason. Within the process of rationalization – man trying to defeat his fate and overcoming his fundamental fears by conquering the natural world around him – fits the idea of preserving oneself against music's fatal attraction, safeguarding oneself against perilous temptations which draw the 'self' from the path of its logic.[4] At stake is the identity of the rational subject. For the sake of his identity, for the sake of saving his identity, Odysseus must take

---

[3]   "In fact, the poem as a whole [the Odyssey] bears witness to the dialectic of enlightenment," is the first sentence of Excursus 1 called 'Odysseus or Myth and Enlightenment' (Horkheimer and Adorno 1973). It should be clear that Horkheimer and Adorno do not understand the term 'enlightenment' as the designation of a more or less clearly marked historical era, broadly running from the mid-seventeenth century to the mid-eighteenth century ('Enlightenment' with a capital 'E'); for them, enlightenment means a through-the-centuries gradually unfolding and still uncompleted developing process in which a necessary submission and objectification of nature in favor of an expanding individuation of man is the most important development. Here, enlightened thinking is a mode of being, a way of relating to the world and humanity's place in the world.

[4]   Furthermore, Horkheimer and Adorno (1973) indicate that, at this point, Odysseus does not remain content anymore with a future dictated by the gods and revealed to him by oracles: he seeks to make his own future.

action in order not to lose himself in the seductive singing of the Sirens; in one way or another, he has to resist their song.

But what exactly makes the encounter with the Sirens' music so self-destructive? In his account to the Phaecian King Alcinous, Odysseus tells him he heard the Sirens say the following:[5]

> Come this way, honored Odysseus, great glory of the Achaians, and stay your ship, so that you can listen here to our singing; for no one else has ever sailed past this place in his black ship until he has listened to the honey-sweet voice that issues from our lips; then goes on, well pleased, knowing more than ever he did; for we know everything that the Argives and Trojans did and suffered in wide Troy through the gods' despite. Over all the generous earth we know everything that happens.

In fact, the Sirens offer Odysseus something an enlightened man should not withstand: knowledge. Horkheimer and Adorno, however, identify this particular allurement as that of losing oneself in the past.[6] Odysseus can know the meaning of the complete past in exchange for his life: "Even though the Sirens know all that has happened, they demand the future as the price of that knowledge, and the promise of the happy return is the deception with which the past ensnares the one who longs for it" (Horkheimer and Adorno 1973: 33). Self-identity is endangered here in a twofold way. First, the enlightened subject who complies with the Sirens' deluding enticement is beyond redemption as he eventually renounces Reason as 'the prime mover.' Reason is threatened by the singing of the Sirens through its irresistible promise of fulfilling desire. Second, the subject is deprived of one of the two poles through which it exists – the future (the prospect of being able to live in a time that has yet to come). As Victor Taylor asserts: "The 'logic' of oneness [the logic of self-identity] implies an economy of ownership in which one seeks security by struggling against dispossession, impropriety, and expropriation" (V. Taylor 1999: 130).

Now, Odysseus desires the experience of risking his identity, his reason, and his putative control over music and nature, but without actually losing it. What is his mythical trick that enables him to hold self-destruction and self-preservation together? According to Horkheimer and Adorno, he is given two ways of escape: labor or aestheticism. The first one he prescribes for his traveling companions. If they wish to remain alive, they should not be able to listen to these musical temptations. Their labor, the rowing, must prevent them from becoming distracted.

---

[5]   As Michelle Duncan correctly notices, Odysseus is the narrator of a story about the Sirens of which he is the single living mortal authority. This provides him with a powerful vehicle for the task of self-invention and opens the possibility of inscribing himself as a hero (Duncan 2005: 3).

[6]   Is it a misreading by both authors that they only emphasize the fact that Odysseus is offered knowledge of everything that happened in the past? From the text it seems clear that the Sirens are also offering to give him insight into the present and the future.

Odysseus himself, eager to listen while retaining control, chooses the second option. Fettered to the mast, he exposes himself to the Sirens' singing. However, in order to 'neutralize' the music's power, he must turn it into a 'mere object of contemplation,' into art. Horkheimer and Adorno claim that art arises as that which mediates between self-destruction and self-preservation. The result, however, is that the productive tension built into the dialectic movement, that is, the irresolvable tension between preservation and destruction, is sacrificed in the safety of the contemplative position.[7] In other words, the enlightened subject maintains his identity, but at considerable cost: Odysseus loses (a part of) himself, in trying to save himself.

Thus far for Horkheimer and Adorno. I would like to resume the question already posed above: what exactly is it that Odysseus, as a prototypical enlightened subject, as a prototypical man of Reason who secures his identity by excluding otherness, has to be afraid of? What is this 'otherness' of music, presented in this myth in opposition to Reason, to thinking, to *logos*? Let us listen to Circe's words again: "The Sirens *by the melody of their singing* enchant him." In narrative terms, their song can only sing, can only do by singing.[8] The Sirens act solely through sound, which means not through language or at least not through the representational part of it. As Michelle Duncan puts it, their song is markedly acoustic or non-verbal rather than literary or transcendent; it imparts a resonance that resides beyond the representational power of language. Its presence is not domesticated, not dominated, not swallowed up by representation. In his retelling of the Sirens' song, it is exactly this resonant touch that Odysseus cannot replicate.[9] He is confronted with the impossibility of representing the magical power of the Sirens' song or of music in general. Odysseus is able to listen and at the same time disarm the power of the Sirens. However, his narrative is unsuccessful in domesticating the Sirens' song (Duncan 2005: 5–6). Duncan's observations resonate in an essay by Dutch musicologist Etty Mulder on music and identity. In exchange for listening to their song, the Sirens offer the prospect of knowledge of both past and future. Mulder reads this as if they present, on the level of their singing, omniscience. In other words, this knowledge does not surpass the musical level and can therefore not be conveyed as and by discursive text (Mulder 1994: 8). Accepting or recognizing a knowledge 'on the other side of language' requires leaving behind one of the ideals of Enlightenment: a world controlled by reason and logos. Is this the light of the revelation versus the light of the Enlightenment?

---

[7] Especially imagination and creativity – that which is normally produced in the dialectic between self-destruction and self-preservation – atrophy in this safe, contemplative position.

[8] The etymological correlation between 'to enchant' and 'chant' is remarkable here.

[9] Just as the Sirens remain forever invisible (the forewarning that marks the ship's proximity to the Sirens is not a vision, but a change in the wind), their sound is never directly present in the Odyssey. Odysseus' representation of the Sirens' song is not a real song, but more a narration, a narrative text (Duncan 2005: 4). Odysseus' report on the Siren's singing can only function as a paratext, acting on the threshold of what will ever remain unsayable.

That which endangers Odysseus, which undermines the self-identical subject position of the enlightened man, is music – insomuch as it eludes any confinement within a discursive order or representational system, that is, within linguistically organized categorical and classificatory frameworks. It is a fundamentally different and alien mode of existence that must be rejected by Odysseus.

While trying to avoid the trap of falling back into a thinking depending on so-called 'transcendental signifieds,'[10] I would suggest calling this for a moment, following German theologian Rudolf Otto, the *numinous*. Although Otto connects the numinous explicitly with a Christian God, I would like to proffer this term in a non-transcendental way – not referring to some otherworldliness or higher principle, thereby avoiding the presumption of and aspiration toward a being-other-than-being in and of the material world. For me, the numinous refers to a "material experience of the material world, which in its contingency and temporality always exceeds any and every consciousness we have of it and any and every organizing structure we impose upon it" (Finn 1996: 160–61). In my opinion, Otto gives occasion to this claim by stating that a careful definition of the numinous is impossible on account of it being absolutely non-rational (not to be confused with the 'irrational') and (therefore) incomprehensible for the reasoning mind: the numinous is an indescribable and unutterable mystery. The 'radical otherness,' that which is quite beyond the sphere of the usual, the intelligible and the familiar, gives occasion to an 'uncanny' feeling rather than a feeling of danger, to a special kind of fear that may be called 'dread' or in Otto's terms the *mysterium tremendum*. Co-existing with this *mysterium tremendum*, Otto distinguishes a power of fascination. This alluring quality of the numinous, a force that is nearly irresistible, he calls the *mysterium fascinosum*. The numinous, combining dread and fascination in a 'harmony of contrasts,' is therefore named by him the *mysterium tremendum and fascinosum*.[11]

It is this numinous working in music which fundamentally disturbs identity. Music is able to temporarily or permanently affect the structure of the ego, to manipulate and disrupt notions of space, time, and individuality. Experiencing music as the numinous means recognizing in music a (Dionysian) power that devours any modernistic idea of identity, a power already present in the historical foundations of our civilization, as we have seen.

---

[10] A transcendental signified is a meaning that lies beyond everything, something that underlies our whole existence, our thinking, feeling, and acting. During the long history of philosophy, many labels have been used to designate such a transcendental signified: Ideal, the World Spirit, Mind, Consciousness, and of course the most powerful and widespread: God.

[11] It seems like Otto's numinous has much in common with what, for example, Edmund Burke called 'the sublime.' Like the numinous, the sublime cannot be explicated, is mysterious, and is both daunting and intensely attracting. Though he distinguishes the numinous and the sublime as separate categories, Otto admits that they exhibit close connection. Because of their similarities, there is a tendency for the sublime to pass over into the numinous and for the numinous to pass over into the sublime.

Through this short meditation on the Sirens, self-identity, and the numinous, I am touching upon something that Mircea Eliade would call 'the magic of the ordinary' and which I would like to call a spiritual experience. As stated above, I am aiming here to understand the experience of spirituality – unlike Otto and Eliade – in terms of "the particular and specific contingencies, complexities, and necessary mysteries of our existence as material beings" (Finn 1996: 160). In my opinion, all experiences, knowledges, values, aspirations, and desires characteristically claimed for a transcendent spirituality can be understood as and in terms of the experience of *being* in excess over (rational) *thinking* (and *vice versa*). They do not refer to a reality beyond the material world but to a reality beyond its categorical frameworks.[12] Experiencing spirituality means experiencing excess without "syphoning [it] off into and for some 'transcendent' space of other-worldliness, of the immaterial" (Finn 1996: 160). A language of spirituality that suggests a transcendence of the material world ignores this vital and dynamic space between category and reality. It ignores the idea that experiences of excess are "the necessary and indispensable conditions of ecstasy, creativity, change, and critique" (Finn 1996: 163).[13] Unremittingly and without rest we should try to give shape to something which never absolutely coincides with what we can show, read, or write. Spirituality, regarded in this way, means a permanent undermining and criticizing of the constructions with which we build our tower of Babel. Spirituality happens in life in the form of a command, a call, or a perspective which adopts a

---

[12]   Already in 1951, Alan W. Watts writes in his *Wisdom of Insecurity*: " If we want to keep the old language, still using terms as 'spiritual' and 'material,' the spiritual must mean 'the indefinable,' that which, because it is living, must ever escape the framework of any fixed form" (Watts 1951: 71). Watts's analysis of the Western world is that everybody and everything has to have its label, its number, certificate, registration, classification. What is not classified is irregular, unpredictable, and dangerous. In his book Watts tries to open up our senses exactly for the unclassifiable which – though it can be represented by the word 'God' – should not be considered as something otherworldly but as the real present in which we live, "which is the unknown in the midst of coming into being" (Watts 1951: 94).

[13]   This line of thinking as well as all the quotes can be found in Geraldine Finn's book *Why Althusser Killed His Wife* (1996), especially chapter 11. I also derived inspiration from Robert Solomon's *Spirituality for the Skeptic* (2002) in which he is searching for a non-institutional, non-scriptural, and non-exclusive sense of spirituality, one which is not self-righteous, not dogmatic, and *not other-worldly* (Solomon 2002: xii). According to Solomon, spirituality involves finding or giving meaning to that which cannot be explained or justified (Solomon 2002: 81). Although I admit that sheer indeterminacy would not reach us and a complete abstraction from every sense is therefore inexpedient, Solomon's use of the word 'meaning' calls suspicion upon itself in that, ultimately, a subject would thus be able to come to grips with what initially seemed forever impossible to grasp. According to me, spirituality can better be regarded as a kind of remainder that is no longer nameable or comprehensible. Blanchot talks in this case about the 'neutre' or 'dehors.' It is the affirmative experience of this 'outside' which I would like to call 'spiritual.'

critical attitude towards the existing and the given.[14] This call and this command are audible in and through (some) music. But they come to us in many different, perhaps unexpected (or even least-expected) voices. As if the Sirens can loom up following a random selection.   *stocastic process?*

The somewhat paradoxical conclusion that can be drawn from this is, however, not that we should get rid of categories, classifications, and representations; cast them off, leave them behind, discard them. How could that be possible in the first place? It is only through our classification grids, our schemes of representation that we gain access to the world, that we can relate to reality, that we are able to ascribe meaning and sense to what occurs to us. The necessity of categorizing, classifying, and representing is inextricably bound up with our existence. But this does not mean that the structures designed by us and available to us to gain access to reality coincide with that reality. These structures always tell us both more and less about what they represent. Surplus and deficit at the same time: reality can never exhaustively be mapped, and every concept, every word, every representation always says more than what it represents, just as it is by definition a generalization, never able to confine itself to the one thing it serves to represent. It is in this humble understanding that there is and that there will always be a space between category and reality that an experience of the spiritual becomes possible, and experience which both feeds upon and undermines the structures with which we try to assure, secure, and insure our existence. And it is on this threshold that music does its work. *Ce qui reste à force de musique.*[15]

---

[14] According to Helga de la Motte-Haber one could still speak about transcendence here. However, its meaning has changed: both the places where the transcendental should be sought as well as the orientations of the transgressions have been altered these days. She calls this 'alternative transcendence' a 'Metaphysik des Diesseits,' a metaphysics of this world (de la Motte-Haber 2003: 291–2). Art and the aesthetic imagination are especially equipped – through their possibility of transforming profane events – to bring out spiritual values that appertain to all of them (de la Motte-Haber 2003: 300).

[15] It is difficult to translate this sentence, this title of a text written by Derrida. 'What Remains Through Music' or 'What Remains by dint of Music' both lack the emphasis on a powerful insistence, a hammering. What Derrida wishes to point out is the affinity between music and a remainder, a remainder of or in a text (text in the broadest – Derridaen – sense of the word) which is inaccessible and unattainable for any possible discourse but which keeps impinging on it. Music as that which escapes every discourse while at the same time being part of it: music as the unheard-of. Music as the experience itself of an impossible appropriation. The most joyous and the most tragic.

THRESHOLD 7
Language, Spirituality, Music

In light of the preceding:

> So-called 'spiritual' experiences, aspirations, and values do not refer to a reality (or Being) beyond the material world but to a reality (or being) beyond its categorical frameworks and any particular apprehension or *sens/significance* we may have of it.[1] They refer, that is, to what I have been calling the *space-between* category and reality, text and context, language and being. (Finn 1996: 161)[2]

Spirituality cannot be described within what Alain Badiou would call 'the state of the situation,' that is, the sum total of instituted knowledges – namings, classifications, divisions, distributions (Badiou 2001: ix).

---

[1] A similar thought can be found in Gemma Corradi Fiumara's book *The Other Side of Language* in which she writes that "an aversion – almost – towards listening to the rich multiplicity of 'reality' seems to be linked with a background of profound fears and to the resulting defensive postures that express themselves in a tendency to reduce knowledge in general to a set of principles from which nothing can escape" (Fiumara 1990: 21). In Threshold 11, I will deal specifically with the relationship between spirituality and listening.

[2] It should be clear that, when speaking about the space between category and reality or language and being, I do not assume a world which is 'a given' and which can then be interpreted in many different ways. On the contrary, I agree with Gianni Vattimo that those interpretations constitute the objectivity of this world. The world is not an object which can be objectively 'known'; rather, it is a place where symbolic systems are produced, a playing field of many fictions. Reality is the result of an intersection and contamination of a plurality of images, interpretations, and reconstructions produced by media that are conflicting among themselves and without a 'central' coordination (Vattimo 1998: 23 and 41–2). My thrust here is that in the categorical structures, which are the results of the interpretative acts, some things remain undiscussed, unseen, unheard. It is not my intention to develop a new series of interpretations which will fill this gap, this space between (by definition impossible). I do, however, wish to pay attention to the fundamental deficit of every category and classification because it is precisely there, in their inadequacies, that I see traces of what might be called the spiritual. Spirituality can be regarded as the deferring movement, a shifting otherness always escaping any categorization, any frame, any name, any thinking. If it is possible to suspend the activity of grasping, the aggressiveness, the usurpation characterizing the regimes of mind, it is perhaps not impossible to become open to traces of spirituality.

However, all this should not be understood as a mere rejection of classifications or orderings. On the contrary: naming and framing causes beings to appear, bringing them into unconcealedness and also offers possibilities to go beyond set metaphysical stipulations. In other words, any system of ordering (language being one of the most powerful) discloses reality as well as keeping beings and events concealed.

The fundamental impact of these remarks is the shift that takes place in the understanding of spirituality from transcendentalism to immanence.[3] It calls to mind a meditation of Lyotard in *The Inhuman*: "The inexpressible does not reside in an over there, in another world, or another time." And it is to this that art (music) must witness (Lyotard 1991: 93).[4] While concepts like 'the world' or 'music' might be understood as being derived through and during the constitution of vocabularies, discourses and their rules, the word 'spirituality' should remind us of their boundaries and conflicts. 'The spiritual' is not a positively definable quasi-entity beyond or above common reality, referring to something otherworldly or the absolute presence of a divinity; rather it functions, in an ambivalent way, as an alien or monstrous turmoil in the margins of a discourse.[5] The value of spirituality is situated precisely in a sensitization of thought for and through that which is not enlightened by it. Spirituality, thus read, is a critical concept or a limit-concept, outside every possible presentation, though it can be implied negatively through a presentation; it has mainly an indicatory value.[6] (Given a positive, specific meaning, 'spirituality' might become a totalitarian concept, whereas I see it as the

---

[3] In *Spirituality for the Skeptic* Robert C. Solomon correctly argues that spirituality regarded as something supernatural too readily projects it away from us. A 'naturalized spirituality' as he calls it is "not opposed to but embraces the material world" and, therefore, "the place to look for spirituality is right here" (Solomon 2002: xvi, 9, and 20).

[4] What Lyotard calls 'the event' in art – the happening as such (*quod*) that precedes subsequent questions about what it is, about its significance (*quid*) – other philosophers connect to sublime or mystical experiences, one of a very few trustworthy forms of sacrality after World War II: not a belief in occult symbols, but a sensory experience in the here and now, a form of divinity not outside but within the phenomenal world.

The transcendent is thus present within the material, not unproblematically, but as a momentary felt 'beyond' in the experience of a limit, a border.

[5] "Aliens always flourish in border country. Creatures which hang around borders, and disrespect their integrity, are traditionally known as 'monsters.' They comprise a species of sinister miscreants exiled from the normative categories of the established system. A species of non-species, as it were. Alien monsters represent the 'unthought' of any given point of knowledge and representation, the unfamiliar specter which returns to haunt the secure citadel of consciousness ... Monstrosity, in fact – and not error – is what most menaces the will to truth, because it is radically heterogeneous to and cannot be accommodated by that will" (Kearney 2002: 119–20).

[6] This conception of spirituality comes close to what Badiou describes as 'the unnameable':

The unnameable is not so 'in itself': it is potentially accessible to the language of the situation, and we can certainly exchange opinions about it. For there is no limit to communication. The unnameable is unnameable *for* the subject-language. Let us say that this term is not susceptible of being made eternal, or not accessible to the Immortal. (Badiou 2001: 86)

Badiou subsequently defines Evil as precisely the desire to force the naming of the unnameable.

opposite, postulating a sustainment of oppositions rather than a violent union.) The transferal from a metaphysical to a critical reading implies that the spiritual, the spiritual as the inexpressible, is no longer hypostatized as an otherworldly quantity, but as somehow present on this side, in this world.[7] In other words, it neither more nor less testifies to the awareness of a boundary; it *is* the boundary, the threshold. Rather than as an ultra-determining reality, the spiritual becomes more accessible when conceptualized as a limit or boundary. This displacement is in contrast to a definition of spirituality through a process of identification.

Although spirituality may involve a sense of the ineffable and the unnameable, and although it lacks apt categories, these are not arguments relieving us from the task of bringing it up. Or, more cautiously formulated, the question we are encountering here is if this way of thinking eventually discharges us from speaking and writing on spirituality, on spirituality and its relation to music. Both spirituality and music are ineffable. "Whereof one cannot speak, thereof must one be silent."[8] Perhaps we should read the word 'must' not as a kind of incitement, something like "it would be better to remain silent." Instead, 'must' could also refer to a fundamental impossibility: "one has no choice but to be silent." If the spiritual, whether or not connected to music, always already escapes any language, any category, any conceptualization, why then this desperate and beforehand prospectless endeavor to speak and write on the relationship between music and spirituality? Spirituality and music meet each other in a space which is inaccessible for language. Both belong to a pre-thematic and an-archic space which is not already (or not yet) pre-dictated, pre-determined, pre-scribed, and thereby foreclosed by language and the various institutionalized relations that organize its meanings (Finn 1996: 155). Nevertheless, poststructuralists and philosophers of language have pointed out the paradox: only *through* language, only *through* categorical frameworks will we ever be able to catch a glimpse of this realm outside or beyond language and its accompanying institutions. To reach the unthinkable through thinking, the unspeakable through speech, the space-between through classifications, the ineffability of spirituality and music through language – this possible impossibility, this paradoxical task, is awaiting us. And through the above-mentioned, it should be evident that achieving this task has only a chance of success if we do not confine ourselves either to the disciplining structures of already existing (musicological and music theoretical) categories or to the categorical imperatives at work in the current discourse on spirituality. Imprisoning the relation between music and spirituality in a (new) category – for example adorned with the fine and promising

---

[7]   Perhaps the term 'metaphysics' could be saved if it is no longer understood as a philosophical discipline in search of the transcendental. As Heidegger suggests in his course *Die Grundbegriffe der Metaphysik* [*The Fundamental Ideas of Metaphysics*], the prefix 'meta' could also be read as turn or swing, as in metabolism. Metaphysics, regarded in this sense, is not a departure from earthly existence; it introduces and starts a process of revolution or change and cuts across the naturalness of ordinary structures.

[8]   Sentence no. 7 [the final sentence] of Wittgenstein's *Tractatus Logico Philosophicus*.

designation 'New Spiritual Music' – only seems to obstruct a possible encounter. My argument is that music and spirituality come to us from the hither side of language and the prescribed and prescriptive categories of sedimented thought, that is, in the gesture of the *énonciation* rather than the signification of the *énoncé*.

The questions are obvious: how then can language provide any contribution in the reference of music to the spiritual? How then to speak of/to/with/around music and spirituality? Or, to couch it in more negative terms, how to avoid, in Heideggerian formulation, a 'vorstellendes Denken,' a thinking that starts from the assumption that beings are in principle close by, accessible, and available. *Vorstellen*: to represent, to make present, to make oneself familiar with something, to master. This thinking opens the door for objectification, making categorizations and classifications possible. According to Heidegger, man should try to free himself (at least partly) from the oppression of this 'vorstellendes Denken,' a thinking articulated in words that are mere denotations of alleged presentable beings, a thinking that is animated by the idea of *adaequatio*, that is, the accordance between judgment and matter or between sign and signified or referent. Heidegger asks us to break radically with this familiar form of thinking in order to be able to open ourselves for 'something' (Heidegger's *sein* or *seyn*) that always already escapes grasping. For instance in *Was heißt Denken? [What is Called Thinking?]* and *Was ist Metaphysik? [What is Metaphysics?]* Heidegger leads us explicitly to a kind of thinking, *real* thinking as he calls it, which is responsive to the unfathomable mystery hidden behind all supposedly solid ground: an 'andenkendes Denken,' which is always permeated by a trace of the inaccessible and unthinkable, of that which causes one to think. To think for Heidegger is not to understand; to think is to be moved, to challenge and to be challenged. This implies that Heidegger is also groping for a language which does not seek to most completely represent the comprehensible but, instead, a language which endeavors to refer to unthought-of dimensions and undecided zones that escape common thinking. Language, however provisionally and tentatively, has its own concealed potential for calling up 'the other,' so Heidegger believes. Language brings up; it brings up what was previously passed over.[9] It makes it possible for something to emerge as something. Language is, as such, 'Dichtung' or poetry: the originally creating word, a projective saying ('Entwurf') of something new within the borders of the approved, the quest for an otherness

---

The word often appearing in Heidegger's writings is the Greek *aletheia*, which Heidegger peculiarly translates as 'unconcealedness.' It should, however, immediately be noted here that, according to Heidegger, this unconcealedness is always accompanied by concealedness. *Aletheia* is an event of disclosing and hiding. Beings do not show themselves from all sides; many aspects and possible perspectives remain obscure. Moreover, one feature of this unconcealing concealedness is that something always comes to us in a transformed way, veiled by a shadow, distorted by a perspective, hidden behind another being. No being is ever fully present.

that can just be evoked within the prevailing frames of thinking.[10] It should be clear with this last remark that for Heidegger this poetry still draws upon the current language.[11] He is not promoting a radically new language, but a language that gives account of the unsayable (the 'saying' as Levinas would call it) within the said, the indescribable within a definition, an 'otherness' within 'the same,' in short, a language on the threshold of the inaccessible and the inexpressible.

It is this 'andenkendes Denken' that might serve as a guide, leading us to encounter traces of spirituality. In light of this, it is significant to note that one of Heidegger's key words comes directly from the language with which we approach music: the word 'Stimmung,' meaning both 'tune' or 'tuning' as well as 'mood' or 'spirit.' Within the complex etymology of this word, the relation between the human mind and the musical harmony of the spheres seems to play an influential role: 'Stimmung' carries with it an age-old body of ideas.[12] Heidegger, however, develops his own interpretation of this word. Traditional theories are based on the

---

[10] "Language is not only and not primarily an audible and written expression of what is to be communicated. It not only puts forth in words and statements what is overtly or covertly intended to be communicated; language alone brings what is, as something that is, into the Open for the first time ... Language, by naming beings for the first time, first brings to word and to appearance ... Projective saying is saying which, in preparing the sayable, simultaneously brings the unsayable as such into a world" (Heidegger 1971: 72–8).

[11] In *On Heidegger and Language*, Joseph Kockelmans interprets Heidegger's 'language' as "everything by which meaning is brought to light *in an articulated way*, regardless of whether it is done concretely, by means of the sentences of a language in the narrow sense of the term, or through a work of art, a social and religious institution, and so on" (Kockelmans 1972: xiii). Especially art reveals what was not yet seen; it articulates the not-yet-articulated. Above all, it brings forth the unusual in the familiar, the inconceivable in the presentation. Through art, things, words, sounds are extracted from a normal, meaningful context, and thus deprived of their intimate familiarity.

Though only a footnote here, this insight is, of course, very important in regards to this project on music. Music is, as such, a relatively autonomous world that cannot be paraphrased totally within a logically discursive language. This makes of music a beckoning sign for the untranslatability of being.

[12] In Threshold 5, I already paid some attention to the work of Joscelyn Godwin who attempts a reanimation of the old Ptolemaic idea of a synthesis between music, psyche, and cosmos. In *Harmonies of Heaven and Earth* (1987), Godwin presents himself with the task of offering the possibility of perceiving harmony everywhere in the universe. Godwin presupposes a higher unity, a higher harmony inassimilable through rational thinking, which connects heaven and earth. Music plays an important role in this junction.

The implicit criticism of Heidegger to thoughts such as these expressed by Godwin is, in my opinion, that one runs the risk of presupposing a meaningfully organized universe in which everything already has its place. The human being would then be able to overlook this well-ordered whole as a neutral spectator. This means, however, that both man and the whole are, regarded in this way, 'vorhandenes,' which implies a misunderstanding of man's 'real nature.'

assumption of an Eternal Truth or an Ultimate Light; by letting music resonate in his soul, the 'listener' can attune himself to those higher principles. According to Heidegger, 'Stimmung' is, to be sure, an adjustment to what is situated outside of us; however, this does not imply an attuning to a universal harmony or higher power. On the contrary, Heidegger's 'Stimmung' refers to a foundationless openness, to a submission to the indeterminacy of being, of the material world. Taking the place of an immutable harmony, eternally identical to itself, Heidegger proposes a dynamic event on the basis of which fundamentally new orientations become possible.

Analogous to Heidegger's 'Stimmung,' albeit more radicalized, Georges Bataille speaks of an empty space, in which a supreme or normative Being is absent and in which there is nothing to go by. Bataille reads Nietzsche's 'death of God' (see Threshold 5, note 21) as the cessation of every rational foundation and the dissolution of an all-explaining center. Similar to Heidegger, Bataille advocates an openness towards the dizziness of a world without God, towards the whimsical uncertainties of existence. Displaying an aversion to what he calls 'the project,' a systematic acting that excludes every coincidence, he argues in favor of the play, a playfulness free of any goal outside the play itself.

Language is for Bataille closely connected to the project, reason, or, as he also calls it, the 'homogeneous order' (see Threshold 5, note 11). In language, we fix beings and schematize the world. Simultaneously, however, one cannot speak about the play, about heterogeneity (as opposed to the homogeneous order), about uncertainties without that language. In other words, one has no choice but to use language in a paradoxical way, that is, to speak in language about something beyond language. Bataille leads the linguistic order to its limit in order to obtain a certain provisional access to that which is suppressed by language. The issue at stake is a writing that can never write what wants to be written but *through* which reality can be called up and presented.[13] Without (this) writing, which will always be tentative and circum-scribing (literally: writing 'around'), 'otherness' cannot germinate at all.

Like Heidegger, Bataille finds here a role for the languages of art in general, poetry in particular. In art, 'something' that escapes every representation can be dramatized. Unlike Heidegger, Bataille emphasizes art's heterogeneity, its loathsomeness and disharmony; in short, its radical loss of meaning, and, following naturally from this, its connection to the sacred.

---

[13]   Somehow this reminds me of one of the most profound little stories in Antoine de Saint-Exupéry's *Petit Prince* [*Little Prince*]. "Draw me a sheep …," the little prince asks the first-person narrator. But the narrator has never drawn a sheep before, and all his efforts are rigorously rejected, one-by-one, by the little prince. "No. This sheep is already very sickly. Make me another." "That is not a sheep. This is a ram. It has horns." "This one is too old. I want a sheep that will live a long time." Finally, his patience exhausted, the narrator tosses off a last drawing, casting out an explanation with it. "This is only his box. The sheep you asked for is inside." To his surprise he sees a light break over the face of the little prince: "That is exactly the way I wanted it," he says.

How does this 'exegesis' bring us once again to spirituality and music? Both 'phenomena' cannot escape language or linguistic articulation; both can only be presented *as* spirituality and *as* music in language. Language is indispensable for both spirituality and music to emerge; it produces, calls up, spirituality and music, spiritual music, new spiritual music. Both 'phenomena' must pass through language in order to come into existence. How, otherwise, could one encounter the spiritual as spiritual and music as music? Both spirituality and music are first of all linguistic categories, inventions even.

However, this does not at all mean that language provides us with full transparency in our contact with these 'phenomena.' On the contrary, at the same time as language calls them into being, it desperately fails in its ascribed duty. In a twofold way, language evokes both more and less. On the one hand, language, being essentially repetitive (words, in order to get meaning, in order to be communicative, must be reiterated), always already says more than it (perhaps) wants to say; it immediately exceeds singularity. It is by definition unable to restrict itself to one particular phenomenon. Language, signs, marks immediately generalize. On the other hand, language always falls short. There is always more to say. In fact, the phenomenon that is initially called into existence by language becomes thereupon unreachable for that same language. It is this infinite deferral, this fundamental impossibility of language to present that which it re-presents, which makes me speak of the space between category and reality.[14]

Of course, neither Heidegger nor Bataille solve this problem. However, both are aware of the creative powers of language alongside its fundamental inadequacies. It is with this double awareness that they derail language, Heidegger by inventing neologisms, Bataille by presenting texts that falter and fail.

Firstly, how can we then encounter spirituality through language, as a linguistic concept? Perhaps by hesitating to call it a concept in the first place. Perhaps it would be better to call it, with Heidegger, a 'Vor-wort,' a pre-word, a word that does not present, but which ushers into a zone where presence can kindle. However, even this is too much. This pre-word does not lead into the zone; it only refers to it. What this pre-word opens up is a domain, a space for the unthought-of, a space wherefrom this unthought-of might address and appeal to thinking.

Spirituality 'is' a surmise, a suspicion that cannot be decided nor understood through thinking. To answer the call of spirituality, one can only follow the traces of this surmise and try to attune to them the available words of one's thinking. Thus, the tentative characteristics of this word imply a helping hand to the concealedness of that whose trace it follows. If, however, thinking follows the traces of that conjecture, then it experiences some support from the arts, from music.

---

[14] "Because it is the use and nature of words and thoughts to be fixed, definite, isolated, it is extremely hard to describe the most important characteristic of life – its movement and fluidity" (Watts 1951: 47).

We are far removed here from the more conventional (metaphysical) notion of spirituality. However, in traversing the opened space, by entering the desert in the desert in order to rethink spirituality, does not mean that I am attempting to prove that the prevailing ideas concerning spirituality are simply wrong. (Studying its workings is anyhow more relevant than proving its un/truth.) Mindful of Herman Rapaport's words, these more accepted notions of spirituality are themselves a consequence of how, in an openness, an errancy occurs that belongs to a metaphysical history of entanglements. Such metaphysical orientations are essential to an openness (the freedom, in itself undecidable, to err and not to err), in which a new idea on spirituality can be said to emerge. Both are intrinsic to the interplay of closure and disclosure. The relation between the 'old' concept of spirituality and the 'new' one conforms to a difference not decidable according to the criterion of being able to distinguish between what is true and what is false (Rapaport 1997: 29).

Secondly, how can we encounter music through language? According to Barthes, a verbal interpretation of music must always draw on the poorest of linguistic categories, the epithet, which also serves an economic function: "the predicate is always the bulwark with which the subject's imaginary protects itself from the loss which threatens it. The man who provides himself or is provided with an adjective is now hurt, now pleased, but always constituted" (Barthes 1977: 179). Through the epithet – "this music is this, this execution is that" – both the hearing subject and the 'music itself' are secured:[15] "the musical adjective becomes legal whenever an *ethos* of music is postulated, each time, that is, that music is attributed a regular – natural or magical – mode of signification" (Barthes 1977: 180). An ethos of music. A home. Barthes directs his essay against the inclinations to put music under house arrest, to give it a clearly marked space, accessible for and compliant to being attributed (linguistically organized) meanings. "It would be better to change the musical object itself, as it presents itself to discourse, better to alter its level of perception or intellection, to displace the fringe of contact between music and language" (Barthes 1977: 180–81). A discourse on music should be able to pay attention to those musical aspects which cannot immediately be connected to meaning, to signification, in short, to everything which is in the

---

[15]   In 'Le plaisir du text' [The Pleasure of the Text] Barthes distinguishes between pleasure, on the one hand, as a consolidating, affirming principle which does not challenge the reader's subject position (a comfortable practice of reading) and, on the other hand, *jouissance*, a force that disrupts, enraptures, precipitating a loss: the historical, cultural, psychological subject is rapt, raped, destroyed, his relation with language brought to a crisis. *Jouissance* is the surreptitious underside of the text, the absolute new that invalidates conscience, the untenable discourse, the exception to the rule, the syncope that bursts out or explodes, and the loss of the signified. It is close to an unwritable fear that splits the subject, the extremes of perversion, a break, a subjective loss; it is an atopia, a-cultural. *Jouissance* presents what it represents: the excess.

service of communication, representation, and expression.[16] In opposition to this functionality (clarity, expressivity, communication), Barthes demands attention for a materiality beyond or before signification, something he calls an inexhaustible *signifiance*, a "site where language works for nothing" (Barthes 1977: 187), where meaning is produced "in its potential voluptuousness" (Barthes 1977: 184) against the attempts at expressive reduction, against what can be said in music.[17]

The track I am following here leads to the following anchorage: he who deals with spirituality, music, and their mutual relation should be a wanderer, repeatedly deviating from the normal, ordinary, lawful course, way, or path. He is not only a heretic who transgresses but also a subversive who breaks the (power of the) law, who strays from the correct path, the right direction, the rule of rectitude, the norm. Having forsaken the straight and narrow and given up all thought of return, the wanderer moves to and fro, hither and thither, with neither fixed course nor certain end. Such wandering is erring – erring in which one not only roams, roves, and rambles but also strays, deviates, and errs. Free from every secure dwelling, the unsettled, undomesticated wanderer is always unsettling and uncanny. He is forever liminal, marginal; he is curiously ambivalent, shifty, and slippery (M. Taylor 1984: 150 and 157).

---

[16] Barthes subsumes everything which is customary to talk about and which forms the tissue of the prevailing cultural values under the denominator *pheno-song*, a term he borrows – albeit transformed – from Julia Kristeva. In *Revolution in Poetic Language* (1984), Kristeva makes a distinction between phenotext and genotext. The former might be understood as a structure that obeys the rules of communication, which presupposes a subject of enunciation and an addressee. The latter, on the other hand, is a process, articulating the unstable and the nonsignifying, experiencable in, for example, textual catches, hesitations, displacements, and exclusions.

[17] In my opinion, it is not so much a matter of thinking in oppositions here. Barthes draws our attention, rather, to 'something' that always already traverses or permeates the significating structures, 'something' that 'precedes' (in a non-chronological sense) any enclosure into meaningful frameworks. Every text (text in the broad sense of the word, regarded, that is, as a system of differences) contains such 'genotextual' traces, just as every text has some kind of structure, some 'phenological' aspects. The created opposition is analytical, not ontological.

Barthes' distinction resonates in Nicolas Cook's differentiation between *actualized* and *potential* musical meaning. (Of course, this distinction of modes cannot be maintained rigidly; it deconstructs itself immediately.) The former, verbal, is constructed through musicology and represented in scores, recordings, and schemata. Works emerge as relatively stable wholes. The latter, sensory, refers to the "inaudibility of [music's] operation as an agent of meaning," leaving room for music's otherness, the opacity of its own voice (Cook 2001: 188–9). Potential meaning always leaves something of itself behind as a remainder whenever an actual meaning is specified.

THRESHOLD 8
Wanderings

"I'm going nowhere. I'm just traveling. I'm on a pilgrimage," says Siddharta to Govinda (Hesse 1960: 87).

Elsewhere in this book, I connected the concept of spirituality to the idea of a permanent displacement (see Threshold 4, footnote 10). In other words, spirituality seems to open a space that can never be occupied because it is, 'by definition,' ec-static, not static, un-stable, enduringly moving.[1]

In line with this view it is perhaps possible to understand the following statement by Michel de Certeau:

> He or she is mystic[2] who cannot stop walking and, with the certainty of what is lacking, knows of every place and object that it is *not that*; one cannot stay *there* nor be content with *that*. Desire creates an excess. Places are exceeded, passed, lost behind it. It makes one go further, elsewhere. It lives nowhere. (De Certeau 1992: 299)

The mystic is a wanderer, a nomad. Spirituality means to leave places, infinitely exploring (inter)territories, always dynamic, always on the move.[3] Therefore, spirituality has to be found *between* places, in the 'in-between.' Like the nomad. Like *a* nomad. Of course, the nomad has a territory; he follows customary paths; he moves from one point to another. He is not ignorant of points. However, the "in-between has taken on all the consistency and enjoys both an autonomy and a direction of its own. The life of a nomad is the intermezzo" (Deleuze and Guattari 1987: 380).[4] Following Deleuze and Guattari, spirituality's nomadism might be clearly distinguished from religion's desire and ability to sedentarize, to establish a solid and stable center.

Writing about a specific mystic wanderer, Jean de Labadie (1610–74), De Certeau seems to endorse this idea. Banished from several West European cities for his controversial thoughts and utterances, Labadie's inner journey was accompanied by geographical ones; an inversed pilgrimage. His writing too is pervaded with a nomadic inbetweenness. It does not effectuate a system; it is

---

[1]   A dynamic notion of the spiritual sharply contrasts with the musical work *Harmony of the Spheres* by Dutch composer Joep Franssens. In this composition four parts frame a fifth, static middle part that (through its setting of texts from Spinoza's *Ethics*) should symbolize 'the eternity of the Divine,' regarded as that which is supposed to be beyond time and space.

[2]   The terms 'mystic' and 'spiritual' are often used synonymously. "Where we speak of 'mystics', a 16th century author instead said 'contemplatives' or 'spirituals'," writes De Certeau (De Certeau 1992: 94). At the risk of being negligent, I will also use both terms interchangeably.

[3]   "Spirituality is a movement, not a state," Robert Solomon writes (Solomon 2002: 37). Following Deleuze and Guattari, one could also capitalize the word 'state' here.

[4]   A striking example of living in the 'in-between' is Iranian Merhan Karimi Nasseri, who lived in the Paris airport Charles de Gaulle from 1988 to 2006. Deprived of his official documents, Nasseri was declared by a French court in 1992 to have entered the airport legally as a refugee and thus could not be expelled from it. The French authorities, however, refused to give him a refugee or transit visa. Nasseri lives in a no man's land, an 'in-between,' standing still amidst perpetual movement and rush.

endless, hastily executed, and pamphletary, a patchwork in which references and theoretical fragments from many religions and in different languages blend, producing a literal and literary ec-stasy. Significantly, the texts are written mostly during the moments of transferal, written in an a-topia. He wrote with his feet, De Certeau says.

> Labadie's wanderings had a direction, a regular orientation: they led him to places where the 'sacramental' conception of space was disintegrating more and more, that is, toward a horizon in which grace was more and more foreign to each place and where, from the view point of the hope of at last localizing sense, extension was more and more 'non-sensical.' (De Certeau 1992: 290)

Labadie's rovings brought him to the margins of religion and religious institutions; he sought out unstable, off-centered places. De Certeau is referring to both Labadie's physical journeys as well as his inner travels, from Roman Catholicism via Protestantism to the foundation of his own quietist sect. Through continuous meditative displacements, he increasingly touched upon or transgressed the thresholds of the official religious doctrines, crossing over to the enemy camp and ending up in a no man's land, his private Labadinism.

He belonged nowhere; no institution claimed him as one of its own. A traveling spirit in search of an actual site which instead turned out to be an impossible, a non-existing one.

What is the difference between this 'traditional' mysticism of The Enlightenment and contemporary spirituality? Implacably, but also with a hint of melancholy, De Certeau concludes that what for the most part still remains, in contemporary culture, is the movement of perpetual departure. However, where seekers like Labadie are still drawn to an impregnable origin or end called God, the current traveler is unable to ground himself in such a belief any longer. What remains is an empty place. He no longer rests upon a foundation or moves toward a goal.[5] His experience maintains only the form and not the content of that bygone mysticism. The attendant desire is described by De Certeau as 'more solitary,' 'less protected,' and 'more radical' (De Certeau 1992: 299).[6]

---

[5]   In aphorism 638 of *Human, All Too Human* Nietzsche writes:

He who has come only in part to a freedom of reason cannot feel on earth otherwise than as a wanderer – though not as a traveler *towards* a final goal: for this does not exist. But he does want to observe, and keep his eyes open for everything that actually occurs in the world; therefore he must not attach his heart too firmly to any individual thing; there must be something wandering within him, which takes its joy in change and transitoriness.

[6]   De Certeau seems to bear a close affinity to Georges Bataille here. Like De Certeau, Bataille is fascinated by the mystics as they speak of the loss of the self and ecstasy. They feel torn and immersed in a not-knowing, something that Bataille is trying to articulate in his philosophy. However, the difference between Bataille and the mystics

So, where is the site of the present-day, spiritual nomad? Conspicuously, in the last part of *The Mystic Fable*, De Certeau shifts the attention to art, poetry in particular. Or, to be even more specific, to the *musicality* of or within poetry.[7] As if contemporary spirituality is situated in art or in one's encounter with art: "the mystic experience […] often has the guise of a poem" (De Certeau 1992: 297)[8] And thus where De Certeau recognizes music's potential spiritual powers – "The music, come from an unknown quarter, inaugurates a new rhythm of existence – some would say a new 'breath,' a new way of walking, a different 'style' of life. It simultaneously captivates an attentiveness from within, disturbs the orderly flow of thought, and opens up or frees new spaces. There is no *mystics* without it. The mystic experience therefore often has the guise of a poem that we 'hear' the way we drift into dance" (De Certeau 1992: 297) – Deleuze and Guattari range music explicitly on the side of nomadology (Deleuze and Guattari 1987: 402). The circle closes.

So, let this 'indefatigable nomadism' be accompanied by some music to match, music by trumpet player Dave Douglas, guitarist Brad Shepik, and drummer Jim Black. The Tiny Bell Trio plays *Songs for Wandering Souls*. Jazz or improvised music. The question is whether these songs are consoling or serving to intensify the experience of roving. Do they make the wandering more pleasant or more deep? Do they distract the minds of the weary traveler or do they affirm a toilsome plodding? Is this music entertaining or an impulse for contemplation? Or both?[9] From the start it becomes clear that these songs are permeated with an absence; they orbit an empty place. The three musicians cannot and/or do not have the intention of discontinuing this absence. Which perhaps creates precisely the opposite effect: precisely by not covering up this lack with all their strength, it appears and becomes present, becomes all the more present, becomes perhaps more present than when it would have been 'actively' present. What am I talking about? What is 'missing' here is the core, the

---

is that according to the latter, the ecstasy should finally lead to God. Their ecstasy is tied to a purpose; their not-knowing must eventually simmer down in a serene and eternal knowing. Their not-knowing is rather a not-yet-knowing. Mystics are not permanently open to undecidability, as they believe in a higher sense. In Bataille's philosophy, ecstasy is meaningless and nowhere can one find a refuge. Whereas the mystics' turmoil leads towards a goal, Bataille's turmoil is, as it were, the goal itself. Transgression, as Bataille presents it, does not open a way to a higher form of knowledge. It sojourns at the threshold between knowing and not-knowing.

[7] "Music and poetry can actually be as one," Novalis writes in *Heinrich von Ofterdingen* (p. 29).

[8] In much the same way, Heidegger describes the poet as a 'Hinausgeworfener' or an erring stranger. A word only gives something to hold on to when it is conceived of as a more or less univocal naming of a basically given thing. When this notion of language is abandoned – as in some poetry – the word becomes completely uncanny.

[9] "This is music that by no means swings in the traditional sense, but rather finds its own pulse and rhythms as do the nomadic spirits who inspired this music," reviewer Jay Trachtenberg writes in *The Austin Chronicle* (September 10, 1999).

pivot of a jazz ensemble: the bass. The base. Providing harmonic support while being a melodic instrument, and belonging to the rhythm section without being a rhythm instrument, the bass (re)presents a certain inbetweenness, the link between accompaniment and lead. Though present in its absence – is it warrantable to call it a manifestation of a 'divine milieu'?[10] – the lacking of the bass/base gives the music more room to breathe, the remaining instruments more space to wander: the drums become a third melodic instrument, the guitar often plays contrapuntal lines instead of chords, and the trumpet explores its depths to accompany the guitar solos. The missing bass makes it possible to deconstruct the border between accompaniment and solo: this dichotomy is no longer adequate here.

Songs for Wandering Souls takes us from the jazz music of Rahsaan Roland Kirk, through some images of the mystical Ghost Ranch in northern New Mexico, to the third of Robert Schumann's five pieces in the popular style (*Fünf Stücke im Volkston*, op. 102), 'Nicht so schnell, mit viel Ton zu spielen.'[11]

Why is this work by Schumann an "infinite source of inspiration," according to Douglas' short commentary in the CD booklet? Is it a tribute to Schumann, who might possibly be considered a wandering soul? Did Schumann compose it for his contemporary Romantic wanderers? Or does the music present some trace of nomadism, leaving a track that could lead us to some 'understanding' of spirituality? The initial harmonies, roughly pendulating between A minor and its mediant C major, which give the first part its somewhat archaic and folky character, do not incline one to such an assumption. A more coordinated analysis also offers few leads (see Ex. 8.1): 'Nicht schnell, mit viel Ton zu spielen' is written in simple Lied form A-B-A. And the melodic development of the main theme is rather conventional, largely in accordance with its vernacular idea. But within this staunch territory, things are roaming. Take, for example, the first six (!) bars. The opening theme is played twice. However, a remarkable change has taken place in the repetition: the theme has been shifted up half a bar, due to an unusually long held note in bar 2. Together with the rhythmically quite unstable fifth bar, the melody obfuscates the 6/8 meter to a great extent. In bars 10–11 this stretching game gets a counterpart: while the harmonic accompaniment is closing off a phrase with a dominant-tonic sequence, the melody does not wait for this ending, (re)starting instead its initial theme exactly at the moment the dominant is struck up, as if it wants to compensate for the 'redundant' g-e leap in bars 8–9.

---

[10] "The divine milieu is neither fully present nor absent but is present only to the extent that it is at the same time absent. It neither is nor is not; it is insofar as it is not and is not insofar as it is. It is not totally positive or completely negative but affirms in negating and negates in affirming" (M. Taylor 1984: 117).

[11] *Fünf Stücke im Volkston*, op. 102 is originally written for piano and cello. Schumann's title of the third piece is 'Nicht schnell, mit viel Ton zu spielen.' Did Douglas make a mistake here by adding the word 'so,' or does this slight deviation from the original title correspond to the divergent performance of the Tiny Bell Trio?

Example 8.1 'Nicht schnell, mit viel Ton zu spielen'

Example 8.1 'Nicht schnell, mit viel Ton zu spielen' (continued)

Example 8.1 'Nicht schnell, mit viel Ton zu spielen' (continued)

Example 8.1 'Nicht schnell, mit viel Ton zu spielen' (continued)

Example 8.1 'Nicht schnell, mit viel Ton zu spielen' (continued)

Example 8.1   'Nicht schnell, mit viel Ton zu spielen' (concluded)

In his interpretation, Douglas even enhances these effects of expansion and shrinkage by playing the A part in a very free, almost rubato style. By not sticking closely to Schumann's text, he follows and honors it in 'its spirit.' With almost nothing to go by, the listener can but stray within a pulse rather than march a clear meter.

On another level, analyzing the form of the piece will cause new problems. In the preceding paragraph, I described the composition as an uncomplicated A-B-A Lied. But where exactly can one locate the transition from A to B? In other words, do the double stoppings in bars 27–48 act as an extensive coda for the A part or as a prelude to the 'real' B part starting with bar 49? In both cases, as coda or as prelude, one could say that these bars are both inside and outside the A and B parts, respectively. These two times eleven (!) bars confront the interpreter with a kind of undecidability, an unnameable no man's land, an in-between, literally an intermezzo. In the Tiny Bell version, this part is even more separated from the preceding and following bars: it is the only part where the guitar is playing the theme, thereby intensifying the idea that the musicians consider it as an individual section. However, in bridging the gap between the A and B part, it is not only separated from them, but at the same time connected to both. This intermediary member is in effect treated as a separable part, a particular part, but also as a nonparticular, nondetachable part, since it forms the articulation between two others (Derrida 1987: 38). Neither one nor the other and simultaneously part of one and of the other. Between things. Intermezzo without being an intermezzo. "*Between* things does not designate a localized relation going from one thing to the other and back again, but a perpendicular direction, a transversal movement that sweeps one *and* the other away" (Deleuze and Guattari 1987: 25). Musical nomadism.

Piece, performer, and listener all seem to become prey to a certain nomadism, a movement of "leaving a system of places for a *je ne sais quoi*, the solitary gesture of leaving" (De Certeau 1992: 291). For the Tiny Bell musicians, this becomes all the more obvious when they enter the sixth step in bar 63. Already on slippery ground as the transition from bar 60 to 61 is marked by a *deceptive cadence*, opening a rather indefinable passage of six bars with the pedal on f, they rift Schumann's proposed unpaved path for an even more unsettling and uncanny soundscape. Submitting themselves to a free play with effects and noises, they become wanderers, moving to and fro, hither and thither, with neither fixed course nor certain end. Unattached to the secluded space of the original composition, separated from its laws, Douglas, Shepik, and Black become vagrants, bums, out-laws, casting the listener adrift as well. Pejorative terms, perhaps, but Mark Taylor carves out a positive meaning as well: "Insofar as the outlaw is not only a heretic who transgresses but also a subversive who breaks the (power of the) law, erring points to the ways of grace" (M. Taylor 1984: 150). Taylor's 'ways of grace' have to do explicitly with his (a/theological and poststructuralist) objections to a thinking that withdraws itself into fallacious securities, thereby excluding otherness.[12] The grace of erring refers to a recognition of the maze, a network of winding and intercommunicating paths and passages, a labyrinth where the postmodern subject affirms the ceaseless interaction of self and other along with a negation of the possibilities to "master otherness and control difference" (M. Taylor 1984: 88). I would also like to stress here an other meaning of 'grace' which undoubtedly resonates in Taylor's text, but is not worked out by him. Grace also indicates 'ornamentation,' that is, to play around or to encircle certain tones, adding sounds and thereby (perhaps endlessly) deferring that which is ornamented. One could say that through ornamentation the deferred tone becomes present in its absence. Otherness permeates and determines the self, as the nomad traverses a territory and the Tiny Bell Trio graciously crosses (out) Schumann's composition by embellishing it through improvisation. Graciously, because they treat the Romantic tradition with respect: where the cadenza is allowed according to Romantic conventions, they start their free improvisation until their slide back into the return of section A.

---

[12]   See Threshold 4.

Ripped from its origin and exposed to strange anachronic influences, Douglas's version of 'Nicht schnell, mit viel Ton zu spielen' drifts in a no man's land, between sameness and otherness, leaving unexpected traces in its effective history. "Marking ... Tracing ... Erring ... Drifting. Drifting ... (A)drift ... (Ad)rift ... Rifting." It is remarkable how Taylor concludes this poetic and associative chain which has served our encounter with Douglas's interpretation of Schumann's composition so well: "A/d/rift toward anonymity ... a common mark of spiritual life" (Taylor 1984: 140). Like De Certeau, Taylor combines spirituality with wandering.[13] Being located in this a-topia, conceivably called the in-between, the wanderer knows of every place and object "that it is *not that*." This should not be understood as a mere negation, a position on the other side of 'that what is that.' It is the unnamable of the in-between, the other of the self–other opposition: a threshold or an interstellar space.

---

[13]   Likewise, in Meredith Monk's opera *Atlas*, travel becomes a metaphor for spiritual quest. In *Atlas*, a journey around the world and the inner voyage of a soul converge. It is interesting that Monk also took steps to include the listener in this quest. While preparing the CD recording of *Atlas*, she decided to omit the last scene of the opera (as performed on stage) because she felt that it offered too much of a closure instead of allowing the listener to remain in motion at the end of the journey.

THRESHOLD 9
The Abyss

"For lack of a better term, let's call it new spirituality." These are the words of Joep Franssens (b. 1955), Dutch representative of the New Spiritual Music movement which finds its most well-known ambassadors in Arvo Pärt and John Tavener. Listening to Franssens' music and reading his interviews, the agenda, well enough known by now, is unarguably confirmed: walls of saturated, harmonic sounds in generally slow tempi, should exclude too much fragmentarization, incomprehensibility, and rationality, blanketed under the term modernism. "I want to communicate with my music," says Franssens, who clarifies this further on as "searching for a harmonic balance" in order to "create an ideal world" which opposes modernism, defined by him as "a position from which reason is overvalued and the emotional appreciation of music is neglected" (Franssens 1997: 22).

It has been analyzed before (see Chapter 4): the aesthetical becomes political and *vice versa*. Who is in, who is out? Who speaks the right language, the *shibboleth*, and who does not?[1] In the interest of fairness, the 1999 Festival of New Spiritual Music in Amsterdam made space for very diverse voices: from South-African Kevin Volans (introducing an African virus into the heart of Western contemporary music) to Mongolian overtone singing, and from Tan Dun's hybrid mix of traditional Chinese and Western classical music to what was announced as the spiritual pop music of the UK's Loop Guru.

Franssens, too, makes no secret of his heterogeneous sources of inspiration, ranging from Stravinsky to Yes, from Steve Reich to Mike Stern, and from Shostakovich to Pat Metheny.

Is it therefore so remarkable that the musical movement of the twentieth and twenty-first centuries which more than any other allied itself with notions of spirituality has been silenced during this festival and is not mentioned at all by this 'post-modern' composer? No, this music is not tonal, not easy on the ear, not restful. But this music can hardly be called rational, conceptual, or academic either. It is based on emotion as well as innovation, contains moments of stasis as well as development, is intuitive as well as based on reason. And regarding communication? Perhaps it does not appeal to the general public, but, at least according to the musicians, it makes direct contact with 'the divine' possible. From the start, this music seems to undermine the carefully constructed oppositions between 'postmodern spiritual music' on the one hand and 'modern rationalized music' on the other.

---

[1]   'Shibboleth' is the password used by the men of Gilead in order to identify and destroy the hostile Ephraimites who could not correctly pronounce the word. As such it became a sign of belonging and association, but along with that, also a sign of exclusion and discrimination. In other words, the very difference from the Ephraimites became intrinsic to the narrative identity of Gilead's men.

Meditations. Om. Interstellar Space. With the music recorded on these albums, John Coltrane shakes the foundations of jazz in the mid 1960s. This upheaval is something that announces itself in 1964 with the release of *A Love Supreme*, or even before, in 1961, with the recording of the *Sound of Music* tune 'My Favorite Things.'[2] In order to rescue his improvisations from the severe straitjacket of fast changing chords and extended harmonic progressions, Coltrane in 'My Favorite Things' founds his playing on scales and modes. Melody is no longer dominated by harmony but is now determined by lengthy soloing on one scale (in this case E Dorian); simple and scanty chord progressions allow each soloist a greater melodic freedom. Based on a constant repetition of the thematic tone material, Coltrane's solos contain a, for that time in jazz history, certain unknown monotony, derived from Indian raga's. However, Coltrane is not simply aiming to create a jazz parallel by using the technical aspects of this Asiatic modal music as a model. The music-technical side would just remain a modish whim if one does not consider the fact that this musical side is a part of and originating from a broader spiritual tradition. In other words, it is first of all Coltrane's spiritual quest that gives the initial impetus to this modal jazz; his musical developments are prompted by and supplemented with spiritual experiences. "During the year 1957, I experienced, by the grace of God, a spiritual awakening which was to lead me to a richer, fuller, more productive life. At that time, in gratitude, I humbly asked to be given the means and privilege to make others happy through music," reads the sleeve notes of *A Love Supreme*, the album where Coltrane for the first time testifies to his spiritual inspiration. Like many other jazz musicians, Coltrane combines elements of Christian, Islamic, Hinduistic, and animistic African religions in order to come to a totally personal belief.[3] From the sixties on, his compositions receive spiritual

---

2   In 'John Coltrane's *Meditations* Suite: A Study in Symmetry,' jazz saxophonist David Liebman distinguishes three periods in Coltrane's career. The early years, roughly 1955 through 1959, embrace his tenure with Miles Davis and Thelonius Monk in which the repertoire consists mainly of standards, blues, and originals, all within a well-defined bebop idiom. Coltrane's modal period begins with the recording of 'My Favorite Things' and the eventual formation of an enduring group with Elvin Jones (drums), McCoy Tyner (piano), and Jimmy Garrison (bass). This period finds its seminal recording in *A Love Supreme* in 1964 which also marks the end of the quartet's basic premises, steady time and at least the semblance of a pedal point or ostinato harmony. From 1965 until his death in 1967, Coltrane develops a freer approach to all the aspects of his music which also leads to a change in the personnel (for example, the addition of saxophonist Pharoah Sanders and drummer Rashied Ali) (Liebman 1996: 167–8).

3   The following biographical data illustrate Coltrane's broad orientation on religion and spirituality: in his youth, Coltrane was active as a communicant in the A.M.E. Zion Church in High Point (NC), the city where he grew up. Later, flutist Yusef Lateef (who changed his name, originally William Emanuel Huddleston, after converting to Islam in the Ahmadiyya movement) redirected Coltrane's interest in religion and philosophy by suggesting that he read the Koran as well as works of Kahlil Gibran and J. Krishnamurti. Saxophonist Sonny Rollins recommended Paramhansa Yogananda's *Autobiography of a Yogi* to him. At the same time, Coltrane became interested in Plato and Aristotle (pianist Joe

titles, personal prayers appear on record-sleeves, and he preaches the Glad Tidings during interviews.[4] However, the most important result is that this syncretism leads to a fundamentally different kind of music. The spiritual quest that Coltrane was on included and prompted the search for new sounds in his music. In other words, the religion was nothing without the music and the music needed the religion as a source of inspiration.

Most biographers clearly separate Coltrane's musical developments from his spiritual awakening or they only reveal the spiritual significance based upon the titles of his compositions.[5] In this discussion, however, I am specifically concerned about the link between the two. Or to make it more concrete, I am interested in the relation between an ever-deepening spiritual commitment and a music that moves more and more to a 'totally free' playing. What is the connection between this increasing religiosity and a music that can, without too much exaggeration, be characterized as excessive? How can we understand the link between song titles such as 'The Father and The Son and The Holy Ghost,' 'Ascension,' and 'Amen' and a playing that transcends the traditions and skills of conventional musical (jazz) idioms? The more Coltrane stands up for his belief, the more inaccessible and innovative his music becomes. No sweet-voiced sounds, no tensionless consonants, no slow and slumbering, long-drawn-out melodies; instead, his later music in particular can be characterized as ultimately corporeal, intransigent, and dissonant. What kind of

---

Knight from the Earl Bostic band urged him to read these philosophers instead of Gibran et al.), Egyptology, Scientology, Cabala, Sufism (this suggestion came from bassist Donald Garrett), and astrology; but he also continued "leafing through the Bible while eating pizza." Due to the influence of Indian sitar player Ravi Shankar, Coltrane started studying yoga and reading the Bhagavad-Gita. And Babatunde Olatunji, a Nigerian drummer who established the Olatunji Center of African Culture in the heart of Harlem, the center where Coltrane played his last concert, recalled that Coltrane asked him about Africa and that he gave him some books on African culture and languages.

　　Hundreds of books to satisfy his need to inform himself about spiritual and religious movements and orientations were stacked on the shelves of Coltrane's apartment.

　　And even though the title of the first track of the *Meditations* album is a reference to the Trinity in Christianity – 'The Father and The Son and The Holy Ghost' – Coltrane explains to jazz critic Nat Hentoff in the liner notes that he "believes in all religions."

[4]　April 1962, Coltrane was interviewed in *Down Beat* together with saxophone and clarinet player Eric Dolphy, who joined Coltrane's band in 1961. While the latter talked more about the technical and interpretive aspects of their music, Coltrane expounded primarily on the music's abstract and mystical qualities (Thomas 1975: 112).

[5]　In *Free Jazz*, Ekkehard Jost writes: "To what extent verbal avowals can be translated into music, and to what extent they can filter into the consciousness of an uninitiated listener through the music, is a matter which need not be discussed in detail here" (Jost 1994: 103). In his formalistic description of certain later Coltrane tunes, interspersed with scanty historical and biographical data, Jost provides little space for references to Coltrane's spiritual quest. J.C. Thomas' *Chasin' the Trane* (1975), on the other hand, focuses in large part on Coltrane's religious motives instead of the 'intrinsic characteristics' of his music.

spirituality is this that needs music – far more than the somewhat awkward words with which Coltrane lets his albums be accompanied – to be expressed, music averse to conventions, free, but informed by brilliant technical skills?[6] What kind of spirituality is this that can only be articulated through an optimal control of the mind as well as, especially, the body, a control achieved not by ignoring or despising the body, but by using it to an extreme extent?[7] Why this battering at what is present, what is available, what is 'vorhanden,' in order to reach beyond it? What is the connection between Coltrane's music and Coltrane's creeds?

Let me formulate my hypothesis cautiously and (therefore) interrogatively: is it possible that, through Coltrane's later music, we can catch a glimpse of a spirituality that cannot be thought anymore within the linguistic and institutional frameworks in which it usually resides, even though Coltrane relies, in a manner almost diametrically opposed to his music, on conventional religious expressions when talking about his spiritual awakening? Listening to his music and relating it to his spiritual quest, I don't hear any teleology or theology; I don't hear a music that arrives, that arrives at a final destination called God. What I hear takes place at the fringes of a gaping hole, a staggering abyss, an empty space. What I hear is a belief in God after the death of God, where and when every explanatory ground has been lost. The effect is a music not of frustration, of sorrow, of mourning, but an affirmative welcoming and joyful nearing of the unknown, of uncertainty, of indeterminacy. Not the retrieval of a last foundation, but the sweeping away of it. All the way. As if Coltrane understands that when he seeks to engage with the spiritual, he must find a position outside of the familiar, beyond any elucidatory agency. The belligerence which can be detected in his music is nothing but the grimness with which Coltrane attacks and transforms the jazz conventions of his time.

In the paragraphs above, I characterized his music as not frustrated. However, by the end of 1966, Coltrane tells Ravi Shankar that he is feeling extremely irritated, that he is still attempting to find something different, but he does not know what he is

---

[6]   According to Swedish saxophonist Gunnar Lindgren,

> … some people like their musical communications in a disciplined manner: systematic, consequences, intellectual control, law and order. This in a Bach fugue is highly pleasing. Others are looking for the undefined: openness, broadened sensibility, intuition, and freedom; for example, the uncertainty of John Cage. Coltrane's music contains both a complicated but consequent form and a dimension of hypnotic and almost metaphysical mystery. (cited in Thomas 1975: 125)

Jost, too, reads the music that Coltrane produces from 1964 onward as a combination of spontaneity, intuition and empathy as well as a definite musical organization (Jost 1994: 86–8).

[7]   In *Chasin' the Trane*, J.C. Thomas compares Coltrane to Charlie Parker. According to Thomas, Parker was a 'high flyer,' ripped loose from his roots, with a lack of personal discipline and a spirit free from constraints. Coltrane, on the other hand, was always in control of himself, conscious of his heritage, and building up his power by degrees (Thomas 1975: 59).

looking for (Thomas 1975: 154). But is this not exactly it: that 'something different' is outside of his knowledge, outside of the categories Coltrane has available at that moment. He cannot name what he is looking for because it *is* the unnamable he is after.[8] And could it not be that his frustration is prompted by the intuition that the moment of knowing will be deferred eternally? That he wants something impossible and paradoxical, namely, to go beyond music, through music?

Coltrane is aggravated, but that does not imply a creative regression or an interruption of the development of new musical thoughts. In *The Inhuman*, Lyotard seems to describe quite adequately Coltrane's state. "Thinking and suffering overlap," he writes.

> If this suffering is the mark of true thought, it's because we think in the already-thought, in the inscribed. And because it's difficult to leave something hanging in abeyance or take it up again in a different way so what hasn't been thought yet can emerge and what should be inscribed will be ... This quite probably defines suffering in perceiving and conceiving as produced by an impossibility of unifying and completely determining the object seen. (Lyotard 1991: 20–21)

Coltrane's music-making *is* thinking, true thinking in Lyotard's sense, attempting to reach beyond the already-known, beyond the established conventions; his improvisations are a form of instant thinking, which means that in his music, that is, in his thinking, everything is questioned, including thought, and question, and the process.[9] Thinking means being in a position of resistance to the procedures for controlling, to reject the known, the schemes, the rules. Coltrane somehow has to accept the occurrence for what it is: 'not yet' determined. It is impossible to prejudge it, and there is no security. "Peregrination in the desert" (Lyotard 1991: 74). Coltrane's musical thinking, his thinking in and through music, is a being prepared to receive what thought is not prepared to think.[10]

---

[8]   In the liner notes of *Live in Japan* (1966), Coltrane himself states that "the truth itself does not have any name on it." In *The Mystic Fable*, Michel de Certeau notes that the term 'mystical' or 'spiritual' becomes "the proper one to qualify any object, real or ideal, the existence or signification of which eludes direct knowledge" (De Certeau 1992: 97). Both Coltrane and De Certeau seem to testify here to a space unreachable by common knowledge and common naming and framing. It is my aim here to investigate just to what extent a connection between a spirituality as described by De Certeau and the (late) music of Coltrane is legitimate.

[9]   "One cannot, consequently, admit the crude separation of sciences and arts prescribed by modern Western culture" (Lyotard 1991: 73). In *More Brilliant than the Sun*, Kodwo Eshun somehow agrees with Lyotard. According to Eshun, science is indeed (and always was) a part of music, though not science in the way we usually define it: "Traditional science still means a depletion, cold scientists, extreme logic and the corny clichés. But in musical terms, science is the opposite, science is intensification, more sensation. Science is rhythm intensified, rhythm estranged" (Eshun 1998: 187). In this way, science then refers to a science of sensory engineering and stimulation.

[10]   Lyotard's ideas around thinking as a "peregrination in the desert," called earlier in his book a state of being open for 'the unharmonizable' or 'the inhuman,' seems an independent

A few months after Coltrane's encounter with Shankar in February 1967, he records *Interstellar Space*, a duo for sax and drums, with Rashied Ali. Within only a few minutes of listening, one hears that the music on this album is uncompromising. It is excessive, transcending every logical explanation, the result of supreme concentration without fixation, that is, without the four restrictions that block an 'open attitude': surprise, fear, doubt, and hesitation.[11] *Interstellar Space* is the ultimate expression of Coltrane's attempt to attain the unattainable. This attempt takes him deeper and deeper toward that empty space, the space *between* the bright spots, the darkness surrounding that which can still be named: inter-stellar space refers to unknown black holes rather than eternal light. This music moves *between* the stars, between anchorages, in a space where the I/eye that surveys, scans, and sees through, is helpless and powerless, a space without identity and stability. His music gives a sound to this space between, a sound most likely not imagined by the advocates of the Harmony of the Spheres.

On 'Leo,' the second track of the album, Coltrane examines the same motifs again and again, inverts them, plays them backwards and upside down, gives them to his co-researcher to hear what he can do with them. It is a constant exploration of the material, offered to Coltrane by himself, through endless studying, through endlessly trying to accomplish the impossible: to unravel the mystery of music, to reach the divine of music and the divine through music. The repeated (and – thereby – simultaneously altered) motifs are alternated with rapid scales and arpeggios, an intensification and further development of his 'sheets of sound' period of the

---

echo of Heidegger's call to rethink thinking. In *What is Called Thinking?*, Heidegger rejects the idea that thinking is ratiocination, developing a chain of premises leading to a valid conclusion. Nor is it conceptual or systematic in the sense favored by the German idealistic tradition (Hegel's *Begriff*). "Thinking does not bring knowledge as do the sciences. Thinking does not produce usable practical wisdom. Thinking does solve no cosmic riddles" (Heidegger 1968: 159). Thinking for Heidegger is dwelling, questioning and putting oneself in question, surmounting the boundaries in which all customary views are confined in order to reach a more open territory, seeking to press beyond systems and concepts (yet with rigor and strictness). "We can learn thinking only if we radically unlearn what thinking has been traditionally" (Heidegger 1968: 8). By exploring and entering new musical areas, by going beyond the traditional ways of thinking within jazz idioms, Coltrane answers Heidegger's call.

[11]   In *John Coltrane and the 'Avant-Garde' Movement in Jazz History* (1986), ethnomusicologist De Sayles R. Grey demonstrates how Coltrane on *Interstellar Space* (more specifically in 'Jupiter'), as in many other compositions, makes use of the so-called 'inverted fourth principle,' developed by pianist Hasaan Ibn Ali. Instead of playing typical chord notes, thirds, Ali plays fourths on top of one of the chord tones. The inversion takes place when one or more of these fourths are transposed an octave down.

By stating that the music on *Interstellar Space* is beyond any logical explanation, I do not wish to say that it is impossible to approach it with the help of some music theoretical tools; on the contrary, they can be quite helpful in gaining access to certain aspects of this music. But this access simultaneously opens and closes the door to other features which cannot be named so easily within this discourse: the intense power, the intransigent pelting, the shrieks that scourge the bodies of both musician and listener, and so on.

late 1950s. However, these extremely fast runs should not be understood as melodic elements. No, their purpose is primarily kinetic or rhythmic; they can best be described in terms of compass and duration, not as a series of individual tones. Rather than melodies, they are spans of sound or sound surfaces. The rising succession of pitches increasingly loses its identity as consisting of single tones. Individual tones can hardly be distinguished; they merge into shapes, into sound contours. And when melodic fragments do materialize, there is no continuity of development.

And Ali? What about the function of his drums here? That function can likewise be seen in terms of an exploration of sound. The abundance of accentuations, superimposed on one another and in part canceling one another out, makes the rhythm gain in tone color and lose clarity. Rhythmically fluid levels of accents replace chains of impulses in which the beat, if not directly perceptible, is at least felt. Ali concerns himself more with providing sonic color than with maintaining a steady background for Coltrane's solos.

By redefining the function for drums, by adding percussion instruments (for example, Coltrane plays sleigh bells at the beginning of all tunes except 'Saturn') and by extracting unconventional sounds from the saxophone (multiple sounds, overblowing, sound surfaces, squeals, and cries – described by Andrew White as 'effected saxophonics,' instrument-specific gestures irreducible to the established ideals of tone as set forth by the European tradition), *Interstellar Space* favors a thorough exploration of tone color instead of elements of music which can be readily symbolized by notation (such as predominantly discrete pitch and harmonic progressions), elements which play a decidedly subservient role. There is a gradual emancipation of timbre from pitch that leads to (a-)melodic structures primarily delineated by changes in color and register. All possibilities of tone coloration are incorporated, partly as a constructive device – when they serve as a means of formal articulation – and partly to provide emotional intensification. In this sense, Coltrane's music embraces both emotion and construction, both intuition and reason (Ake 2002: 138–9; Jost 1994: 90–100).

It is doubtful if the creation of *Interstellar Space* dissolved Coltrane's frustration. It is more likely that this album is just another example that he cannot reach the spiritual, that he cannot reach the music. The result: hating music.[12] Not only a hatred towards music: music's self-hatred is articulated here as well. A hatred towards music that finds expression in music itself. The music obsessively challenges itself; it must unremittingly underscore that it does not succeed in evoking what it desires to evoke. In that sense, *Interstellar Space* presents a music that expresses what cannot be expressed and is therefore forced to undermine itself. This music criticizes itself, expresses its disharmony without transforming itself into beauty

---

[12] 'Hating music' alludes to a book by Bataille called *Haine de la poésie*. (Later the title was changed into *L'impossible*.)

or into a meaningfully articulated, harmonious form; it is the radical otherness of a system, as Derrida formulates it in 'Economimesis.'[13]

In *More Brilliant Than the Sun*, Kodwo Eshun writes that Coltrane's music in the sixties "is not so much listened to as withstood" (Eshun 1998: 170). Coltrane turns jazz into 'energy music': his primary focus is on the exploration of textures, on the possibilities of sound, rather than on the construction of organizational unities. His music is about materiality, a material and corporeal spirituality,[14] with speed and volume as energetic forces, circuits of spiritual vibration, moving and amplifying the cosmic program that operates the human (Eshun 1998: 174).[15] Energy music: for example by dourly repeating the same motifs over and over again (as in 'The Father and The Son and The Holy Ghost' from the *Meditations* Suite), motifs that are impudently tonal – with the fifth as a pickup to the first, second, and third degree of the scales. What saves this simplistic melody from sounding trite is the non-matching harmonic accompaniment of the bass and piano as well as the flowing, nonmetrical rhythm underneath (Liebman 1996: 169). While the melody is flagrantly diatonic, the harmonies as well as the improvisations are nontonal,

---

[13]   Shankar never understood that this 'hating music' had everything to do with Coltrane's spiritual quest. After attending a concert at the Village Gate, Shankar remarks that he can not understand the turmoil in Coltrane's music. The turbulence distresses him (Thomas 1975: 141–2). Contrary to Shankar's opinion, I would like to propose the idea that it is precisely this (ostensible) disorder which can reveal something of the relation between music and spirituality in Coltrane's work.

[14]   How far are we removed here from what Peter Dykema and Karl Gehrkens write in 1941 in *The Teaching and Administration of High School Music*:

> Swing music – which is merely a highly emotionalized style of playing jazz, and to which we are in no sense objecting to as a legitimate type of human experience – is primarily physical. It induces violent physical movement – note the jitterbug. It is 'fleshly' in its conception. *It does not lead toward the spiritual.* It is 'good fun' at the time, but it does not yield abiding satisfaction. To use such music in the school as a substitute for serious music is to cheat youth of a highly important experience which has the possibility of assisting in the development of spiritual resources. (Cited in Ake 2002: 117–18, my italics)

[15]   Writing around Coltrane's 1965 album *Om*, Eshun remarks: "If Sound is Mystery, then Volume is Holy and Noise is a Blessed State." 'Om' is the Hindu access code to the sonic origin of the universe. Coltrane's *Om*, with the whole group chanting verses from the *Rig Veda*, the earliest of the four Hindu religious scriptures, is also a serenade to Ohm. Close-miking expands the noise spectrum into the quietude of meditational jazz, crackling with the instant archaism of 'primaudial' sound: the transient tones of bell trees, woodblocks, cymballic susurration, a desolate calm. You're inside the storm (Eshun 1998: 172). Although it contains several elements of Eastern religion, *Om* also opens up to the idea that Coltrane's version of God might not be the God normally associated with the world religions; his 'God' is not limited to the denominational name. Coltrane's God is *Om*, is musical, is sound exploration (one of the meanings of Om is "all possible sounds that man can make vocally" – see the sleeve notes of the album of the same name).

releasing tension through counter-tension, not horizontally, that is, following a time sequence, but vertically, simultaneously audible.

Of course, David Ake is right when he states that to understand Coltrane's musical onslaughts as 'spiritual' rather than 'angry' has much to do with the discourse surrounding his music. It would be hard, if not impossible, to prove that there is anything inherent in the nature of extended saxophone techniques that triggers ecstatic states in musicians and listeners (Ake 2002: 141–2). The same argument would apply for any meaning we attribute to music (in Ake's case, also the designation 'angry'). However, in my opinion, this does not relieve us from a certain obligation to take the intended relation between Coltrane's later music and his avowals concerning his spiritual quest seriously. Likewise, the more Coltrane is testifying to his religious inspirations, the more his music becomes relentlessly questing, not easy or comfortable by any means, a music that develops analogously to Coltrane's 'inner journey,' a psychic as well as musical dissection in which every nerve is laid bare (see Pete Welding's remarks in Ake 2002: 141).

That is why I call this hating music, corporeal and dissonant, uncompromising and yet uncertain, innovative and yet clearly founded in a tradition, blasphemously testifying of the sacred and the spiritual, profanely giving evidence of the divine and the universe. It signifies by what it takes away. Describing the relationship between this music and the concept known as spirituality, one can only resort to what in linguistic terms is called an *oxymoron*, a trope so well-beloved among early mystics.[16]

---

[16]   In Diego de Jesús' (1570–1621) theory on spiritual phrases, the mystic word is whatever cuts the body of the mother tongue. It is recognizable by the 'cleft' words it produces.

> How will we put order, or limits, or text, or means in the terms by which we must explain so lofty a thing, wanting everything that is immense and unsayable to be subject to the ordinary rules, without exceeding the common phrases and guarded terms of the schools of disciples and masters, of arts and manners that can be taught and known?

Diego asks rhetorically. And he continues:

> The mystic has permission [...] in order to enliven and emphasize, to make its incomprehensibility and loftiness known with terms that are imperfect, perfect, hyperperfect, contrary or noncontrary, similar and dissimilar, as we have examples of all that in the mystic fathers, especially in Saint Dionysius the Areopagite [...]. In order to declare it in inadequate terms, or purposely going beyond the common ones, after having imbued them with furor, irrationality, and insensibility, all of that being understood beyond the understanding, as he says, coming to treat of the quiet they enjoy, he says: "Immanem quietem." That they have a 'cruel repose.' The most dissimilar and contrary thing to quiet that can be. Yet he did it with a divine counsel, since, by what he said of 'quiet' he removed the imperfection of 'fury,' and in saying 'cruel and furious quiet,' he declared the perfection and excellence of this repose. For whoever hears 'quiet' unqualified seems to be contemplating something lazy, insipid and cold, lax, of low

It is impossible to make the unsayable subject to ordinary rules, impossible not to avoid common phrases. However, it is just as impossible not to use the language available to us. What is needed is a practice of detachment, a denatured language. As Jean Baruzi writes in his 'Introduction à des recherches sur la langage mystique' in 1932: "The mystic language emanates less from new vocabulary than from transmutations performed within the vocabulary borrowed from standard language" (cited in De Certeau 1992: 141). As 'creative daring' it drifts toward dissimilarity. The deviation creates strangeness in the order (or the 'proper') of language. "It is exit, semantic exile, already ecstasy" (De Certeau 1992: 142).

To create strangeness in language through language. *Rewriting* is the word Lyotard proposes, referring to a withdrawal from "the law of concept, of recognition and prediction" by "unexpected and 'fantasy' associations" (Lyotard 1991: 34–5). By means of an oxymoron, for example, a figure of speech combining incongruous or contradictory words. Or, more broadly, something that is made up of contradictory or incongruous elements. Could we consider Coltrane's music as oxymoronic? If so, I would suggest the characterization 'restricted freedom.' Let's return to *Interstellar Space* once more. By eliminating the chordal instruments, Coltrane gains a more or less infinite harmonic freedom. Exchanging Elvin Jones for Rashied Ali frees him from a too narrow rhythmic straitjacket; more than Jones, Ali likes to stretch and contract the time, constantly shifting his rhythmic accents and concerning himself less with basic pulsation. The result is an ecstatic or excessive dialogue with no harmonic, melodic, or rhythmic restraints.

---

value and mediocre perfection. But whoever adds that it is 'cruel and furious,' already removing the imperfection of fury by 'quiet,' communicates the power, perfection, and intention, and, so to speak, the unbearable and incomprehensible excellence of that 'quiet,' and the excess that it has over the imperfect that occurs within ourselves … Hence Hugh of Saint-Victor is quite right in saying: "Not only are the dissimilar figures probable, because they show the heavenly excellences, but also because they withdraw our minds from the material and corporeal figures more than similar figures do, and do not permit us to rest in them" …. Terms that are imperfect and, if one must say it thus, vicious by excess, declare much better, like saying 'furor' and 'pride'. For we see plainly that the pettiness, the evil they represent when applied to ourselves, is very far from God: And thus to take these terms that mean excess and disordered, unregulated and unreasonable things, is to admit that the good to which we apply them is a pure, very perfect good, such that it all surpasses all order, all means and natural agreement, and everything reason can attain. (Cited in De Certeau 1992: 139–40)

Above, Kodwo Eshun gives a contemporary example of an oxymoron when he describes Coltrane's music as an example of material or corporeal spirituality. And drummer Roy Haynes described his playing with Coltrane as "a beautiful nightmare" (cited in Thomas 1975: 119).

Another oxymoronic remark appears in a review by Whitney Balliett in *The New Yorker* of the album *Giant Steps*: "That ugliness, like life, can be beautiful is the surprising discovery one makes after attempting to meet the challenge offered by Coltrane" (cited in Thomas 1975: 89).

And the shrieks and growls that can, for example, be heard in the middle parts of 'Jupiter' make clear that Coltrane is also exploring the physical possibilities of his instrument. However, 'Jupiter' is basically built around a single motive, a minor third up followed by a half-step down.[17] The initial theme (the main theme?) is a triple repetition of this motive, each time a perfect fourth higher than the previous one and followed by a secondary contrapuntal line (see Ex. 9.1).[18]

The same motive is used as an individual trichord in descending chromatic figures. In 'Jupiter,' Coltrane thus pursues a classic variation technique based (almost) entirely on the development of motive (see Ex. 9.2).

Example 9.1 'Jupiter', the theme

Example 9.2 'Jupiter', variations on the motive

---

[17]   The following modest analysis is informed mainly by unpublished notes of Professor Steven Block. I wish to thank him for sharing his knowledge and expertise with me.

[18]   Jost calls this stringing together of two phrases self-dialogues, simulated polyphony, or call and response patterns, such as occurred in the earliest forms of religious Afro-American music (Jost 1994: 100).

This is all the more enhanced by the overarching form of the piece: ABABA, a small rondo form (see Table 9.1).

The A sections are constructed from the motive (the central A section being different from the outer A sections as it has no complete statement of the theme), whereas the B sections feature rapid, repeated, descending scalar runs, the second time followed by non-pitched use of the tenor played at both extremes of its range.[19] However, the B sections also manifest a structural significance: the opening B section, for instance, presents diatonic scalar runs, initiated from A♭, more than a dozen times before they are followed by yet another dozen runs starting from C♭ (A♭ can be considered the overall tonal center of 'Jupiter' – the piece begins with a theme on A♭, and this theme returns at the end of the piece at the same pitch level). The corresponding B section features the same motion of a third from A♭ to C♭.

Table 9.1   'Jupiter', formal division

SECTIONS	SUBSECTIONS	SYSTEMS	MUSICAL MATERIAL
A	a	1–3	6 statements of theme on A♭
	b	(3) 4–5	Chromatic descent from D4-A3
	a'	5–7	2 statements of theme on A (B♭♭); 1 statement of theme on A♭ with codetta (G♭-B♭♭-A♭)
B	c	8–16	Repeated descending scales.
A	a"	17–27	Oblique statements of the theme.
B	c	28–36	Repeated descending scales.
	d	37	Continuation of repeated descending patterns in the highest range of the tenor saxophone counterpointed against quick low-range punctuation of A♭2 and B♭2.
	b'	38–41	Chromatic descent from D♭5 to C♭3 which returns to close on C♭5-B♭♭4-A♭4 as the theme returns.
A	a	42–43	3 statements of theme on A♭
	b	44–48	Chromatic descent from E♭3-B♭2
	a'	49–51	1 statement of theme on A♭ (which is initialized by B♭3) followed by 3 statements of theme on A♭ and coda (G♭-B♭♭-A♭)

---

[19]   "If 'striving toward a higher level of existence,' suggested by Coltrane's titles and texts, has any programmatic expression in his musical content, then it is here, in these insistent and obstinate sequences, whose emotionalism goes far beyond what can be formally notated … As a rule he begins in the low register with what is often a short phrase, and then leads or drives it upward with immense persistence, via many a roundabout phrase and with a steady rise in dynamics, until it ends at last in shrill overblown sounds" (Jost 1994: 101).

Finally, using Schenkerian analytical techniques, it can be shown that there is a consistent development of long-range voice-leading through all sections of 'Jupiter,' a structural design predicated on the small three-note motive in its original manifestation A♭-C♭-B♭ (see Ex. 9.3).

Example 9.3 'Jupiter', structural design

Example 9.3 'Jupiter', structural design (concluded)

I think it is inappropriate to conclude that Coltrane undermines and rescinds his newly acquired freedom by accomplishing a cohesiveness at so many levels of 'Jupiter's' structure. Coltrane's (spontaneously) created webs of development from the use of nested motives to the fulfillment of long-range structures never obstruct his desired freedom, as the structures are nowhere imperative, but emanating from that same freedom. The oppositions blur, the binary forms with which Western logocentrism approaches reality fail, the music reaches beyond a commonly used vocabulary. With this I do not wish to say that Coltrane's music should be regarded as a medium of exaltation and elation, a medium for reaching beyond music to a spiritual state in which music is no longer necessary. It is precisely *in* or *through* this oxymoronic music that we can catch a glimpse of 'something' that – "for lack of a better term" – could be called spiritual.

"It is exit, semantic exile, already ecstasy." But Coltrane's ecstasy is no exalted raising of the eyes; his is rather a rooting in the earth, a staring in the abyss. Not lead by a search for his own greater comfort, he might be described as a nonviolent anarchist, deconstructing the claims of historically developed and accepted ordering systems, rather than as a defender of the unassailable character of certain 'Values.'[20] And this applies both to his music as well as his spirituality.

"The apostle must leave God for God": a phrase current in The Society of Jesus, a well-organized group of 'spirituals,' French Jesuits, around 1630. As De Certeau explains it, this should be understood as a criticism against institutionalized religion which had transformed prayer into obedience and had even put itself in the place of God. For De Certeau – "leaving for a moment the field of history" – this expression unveils a schism between the God of a society at work, transformed into an ideology and an institutional program, on the one hand, and a God who speaks, transformed into extraordinary devotions, on the other (De Certeau 1992: 257–9). The qualification that is pertinent from a spiritual point of view is not one derived from an institutional position. Although the seventeenth-century mystics put themselves in a different position from that of the Church, they claim nonetheless to bear witness to the same God. "They have to prove, at one and the same time, that they speak from a different place (as 'mystics') and that they draw on the same inspiration (as 'Christians')" (De Certeau 1992: 181). More than three centuries later, Coltrane expresses a similar idea with regard to his music: "I've found that you've got to look back at the old things and see them in a new light" (cited in Thomas 1975: 99). That this 'new light' is dark, almost black, in any case obscure, should only confirm the oxymoronic character of Coltrane's search to connect music and spirituality.

One last remark is necessary. One last remark, hasty and rudimentary.

According to me, the emphasis on technical abilities and the extreme corporeality of his music do not turn Coltrane into a ruler and commander. He does not possess 'his' music; he is not mastering it, leading it with full consciousness in the desired direction. On the contrary, he is the obedient and the listener. Coltrane knows that in order to speak truly, one has to listen and in order to think truly, one has to be willing to receive. Listening is constitutive for speaking. Speaking is at the same time listening. In other words, truly speaking is listening from the inside out, as speaking is listening to the language we are uttering. This kind of listening precedes all speaking.[21] Coltrane's creative work does not stem from surgent feelings and brain waves; rather it is true obedience, based on the ability to listen.

This should not be understood as a complete change from the active to the passive. Instead, it can be thought of as a state of *passibility*, a state which requires

---

[20]   It is not without meaning that I am paraphrasing here Gianni Vattimo's words in *Belief*, cautiously describing a 'true Christian' (Vattimo 1999: 92).
[21]   Words of similar import can be found in several places in Heidegger's *Unterwegs zur Sprache* [*On the Way to Language*].

both an active and a passive attitude. It is passive because the listening I am aiming to describe can be read as a waiting for the advent of 'the other' or 'otherness' (spirituality as a process). Yet it is necessary to prepare for this advent, to make this step to let the other come, "to allow the coming of the entirely other" (Derrida 1989: 55).[22]

Coltrane's state of passibility, neither active nor passive and, simultaneously, both active and passive, can be considered as a making space for the event, a space where the event can take place. It opens up the possibility that something can happen. However, what is happening is not at all something that first needs to be controlled, to be programmed or grasped by a concept [*Begriff*] (Lyotard 1991: 111). If I am allowed to adorn this with the name spirituality, it should be clear that (this) spirituality has no solid ground; it is bottomless, abysmal, a concept of the divine after 'the death of God,' that is, after the loss of any explanatory basis.

The question is if the state of passibility, above ascribed to Coltrane, can take other shapes. In order to investigate this question, I turn – perhaps surprisingly – to 'the high priest' of the new spiritual music movement, Arvo Pärt.

---

[22]   "When someone is searching," said Siddhartha, "then it might easily happen that the only thing his eyes still see is that what he searches for, that he is unable to find anything, to let anything enter his mind, because he always thinks of nothing but the object of his search, because he has a goal, because he is obsessed by the goal. Searching means: having a goal. But finding means: being free, being open, having no goal" (Hesse 1960: 128).

THRESHOLD 10
Silence

B ooM, boom, boom, tock ... Boom, boom, boom, tock ... Boom, boom, tock, boom ... Boom, boom, tock, boom ... Boom, tock, boom, boom ...

Arvo Pärt's *Sarah Was Ninety Years Old* begins with an extremely simple percussion solo, lasting more than five minutes.[1] Four quarter notes – three on big drum, one on tom-tom – followed by a fermata which lasts approximately three quarter rests before the percussion starts again (see Ex. 10.1).

Example 10.1 'Sarah Was 90 Years Old', percussion part 1 © 1991 by Universal Edition A.G., Wien/UE 30300

Boom, boom, boom, tock ... more than five minutes of isolated percussion sounds in a desert of silence before two male voices release themselves in short phrases emanating from a (non)audible emptiness, an emptiness reinforced once more by the echoes the voices leave behind (see Ex. 10.2).

Sounds on the verge of the audible. Sounds surrounded by silence. From the figure of sound to the ground of silence which is its condition of possibility. Or *vice versa*. Silence surrounded by sounds. From the figure of silence to the ground of sound which is likewise its condition of possibility.

---

[1]   As Paul Hillier (1997) suggests in his book on Pärt, this bare percussion could be a reference to the *semantron* (a wooden block struck with a wooden mallet). More ancient than church bells, the instrument came into use during the early centuries of Christianity, summoning believers to prayer. However, the summons of the semantron is not insistent; it is only an encouragement: come – if you wish. The onus is upon the recipient. Could the same be said of Pärt's music? Can the beginning of *Sarah* ... be regarded as an invitation to the listener to open himself for that which comes to him? These and other questions will guide this chapter.

Example 10.2 'Sarah Was 90 Years Old', tenor voices part 2 © 1991 by Universal Edition A.G., Wien/UE 30300

*) ⌒ = ♩·

Another oxymoron (see Threshold 9) seems to be the best way to describe this work: silent music.[2] Listening to *Sarah Was Ninety Years Old* reminds me of Schönberg's words in his preface to Webern's *Six Bagatelles* for string quartet opus 9: "Möge Ihnen die Stille klingen!" May silence sound to you – to you, the

---

[2]   An oxymoron makes words say what they do not literally say; they are tormented. The terms combined belong to heterogeneous orders. Moreover, the oxymoron belongs to the category of the *metasememe*, which refers to something beyond language; it makes a hole in language and roughs out a space for the unsayable. Situated at the juncture of two worlds, it is language directed toward non-language (De Certeau 1992: 143).

'Silent music' – the term has already been used by the Spanish mystic Juan de Yepes, better known as John of the Cross (1542–91) – is of course not only reserved for so-called 'classical' music. The music from the album *I Have the Room Above Her* by guitarist Bill Frisell, saxophonist Joe Lovano, and drummer Paul Motian comes to my mind. This delicate music, permeated with a certain laziness or boredom, makes silence audible. For me this is achieved primarily through Motian's drumming: he exchanges clear rhythmic patterns for coloring and brushing cymbals, creating a rustling through which so many other sounds, existing or nonexistent ones (fabricated or invented by the listener's inner ear), can loom up. Frisell's playing is often reduced to just a few notes, their scarcity creating a space in which they are confirmed in their contact with the tones already present. Full chords are rare; some bare notes serve in their stead to support Lovano's melodic lines or to provide them with a certain tartness. The almost childlike tune 'Odd Man Out' is a good example; this simple song based on only two chords becomes a hazy snatch in which more is suggested than played, thereby creating space for that which is absent, un-heard, inaudible.

'believers' of this music. Like Webern, Pärt lets silence sound and brings sounds to silence. Like Webern, Pärt makes us aware of the silence *in* the sounds.[3]

Boom, boom, boom, tock … Boom, boom, boom, tock … Boom, boom, tock, boom … Boom, boom, tock, boom … Boom, tock, boom, boom …

If there is a single (classical) musician whose works are invariably connected to some kind of (new) spirituality, that person is Arvo Pärt (Estonia, 1935). No biographer, no musicologist, no journalist ever manages to avoid mentioning the spiritual aura surrounding his music from the late 1970s onward.[4] Pärt epitomizes the movement known as 'New Spiritual Music.' His music – often described as a contemporary Northeast European mixture of medieval music, Orthodox Church songs and minimalism – accommodates everything the advocates of New Spiritual Music consider as essential characteristics: tonality (or modality), slow tempi, stasis, simplicity, repetition, and tranquility.[5] After the dark years of modernistic musical navel-gazing, this is once again communicative music, as the sales of CDs and the great surge of people towards the concerts give evidence of.[6]

---

[3]   Perhaps there is a fundamental difference between Pärt's compositions and the works of John Cage, although both exuberantly deal with silences. Whereas Cage makes us aware of the fullness of silence – silence always already filled with sounds – Pärt makes possible an encounter with the emptiness of and within sounds – sounds always already filled with silences. Both Cage's and Pärt's works, however, make it possible to experience that "at the heart of Eros and composition […] there is still drifting, excess, annihilation of the regulated" (Lyotard 1984b: 92).

[4]   From 1976 onward, Pärt commenced a new episode in his musical life after a compositional silence that lasted for several years during which he studied Gregorian chant and separated himself from all other musical life, especially the modernistic tradition in which he had worked so far.

[5]   Almost the same description would cover the music of John Tavener (London, 1944). Tavener's (musical) world, however, is completely bound up with the Orthodox Church; it tacitly implies that you can only engage with it fully by embracing the Orthodox faith. With Pärt, such imperatives are lacking.

[6]   According to Hillier,

> Performers of Pärt's music experience something not so common these days [the late 1990s]: the excitement of presenting new music to a wide audience and discovering that the lines of communication are completely and appreciatively open … [This music] clearly answers a strong need in many people – a spiritual as well as musical need. (Hillier 1997: 206)

Hillier's words seem to be a resonance of what David Clarke wrote in 1993, analyzing Pärt's work: "Here at last is a music that reopens the communication channels, offering tonal purity and simplicity of design. What's more, its religious aura clearly has a strong allure for a secularized culture that no longer has any collective way of articulating the spiritual" (Clarke 1993: 680).

In the previous Thresholds I have tried to rethink the idea of spirituality which is primarily reassuring, human, and attainable through or with the help of music.[7] And I am investigating my observation that music and (post)modern philosophy testify to other readings, to other interpretations that incline towards an emphasis on insecurity, undecidability, and the simultaneous occurrence of oppositions, always lurking in the fringes of the discourses around spirituality. Paraphrasing Marguerite Duras, I would say that connecting music and spirituality offers routes to whoever "asks directions to get lost" and seeks "a way not to come back." Down the paths or ways of which so many spiritual texts speak roams the itinerant walker, possibly accompanied by music. Or as De Certeau puts it: "The 'true' mystics are particularly suspicious and critical of what passes for 'presence.' They defend the inaccessibility they confront" (De Certeau 1992: 5). Spirituality in this sense resembles what Mark C. Taylor calls 'the divine milieu,' a middle way that can never be contained, captured, or caught by any fixed pair of terms. Consequently, the milieu – marking "the liminal time and space where marginal passengers always roam" – is at all times para-doxical (M. Taylor 1984: 112 and 115).[8] Here, 'para-doxical' should not be understood so much as meaning contrary to received opinion; rather it denotes something that goes against normal speech or common language, subverting any thinking that bases itself on alleged clear-cut classifications and oppositions. The milieu embodied in music and inscribed in/by writing is spiritual insofar as it is the creative and destructive medium of everything that is and all that is not.

Proceeding along this line of thinking, the embracing of Pärt's work by the New Spiritual Music movement and my (hyper)critical rereading of the spiritual should not and does not result in the conclusion that his music must be excluded from a poststructuralistically informed concept of spirituality as suggested above by De Certeau and Taylor. The question which, however, does arise is how the relation between Pärt's music and the idea of spirituality I propose can be understood. In other words, how is this music able to establish an encounter with traces of what might be called 'an other' spirituality?

Boom, boom, boom, tock … Boom, boom, boom, tock … Boom, boom, tock, boom … Boom, boom, tock, boom … Boom, tock, boom, boom …

---

[7]   The qualification 'human' is here meant to refer to a reversal that is, according to me, taking place in the 'usual' discourse on spirituality, a reversal of the assertion in Genesis 1:27: "So God created man in his own image, in the image of God he created him." In the humanized version of spirituality, one might conclude that the image of God is created after Man in order to make it/Him comprehensible, conceptualizable, even within reach.

A similar idea can be traced back to Ludwig Andreas von Feuerbach's *The Essence of Christianity* (1841).

[8]   "The divine milieu is neither fully present nor absent but is present only to the extent that it is at the same time absent. It neither is nor is not; it is insofar as it is not and is not insofar as it is. It is not totally positive or completely negative but affirms in negating and negates in affirming" (M. Taylor 1984: 117).

Initially the composition *Sarah Was Ninety Years Old* bore another name. Slightly diverging from *Sarah* ... as recorded on the CD *Miserere*, Pärt endued it with the title *Modus*, a word usually translated as 'way' or 'manner' but also meaning 'bound' or 'limit.' The music is comprised of the sparsest of textures and hovers between repetition and variation.[9] Every phrase is really the same said in another way. And yet the continuity acts as if something else is happening. As a constant repetition of the non-identical, at the edge of perceptual difference, this composition is a manifestation of the in-between, for example between linearity and stasis, between freeze and vibration. Patterns come and go, without development; intensities without a past or a future.[10] Because of this, the concept of time – rhythmic progression, dialectical organization, and formal construction – loses its structural meanings. According to Paul Hillier, *Sarah* ... presents in alteration two distinct sequences: one of rhythmic and one of melodic patterns – the rhythms having no designated pitch, the pitches little or no rhythmic differentiation (Hillier 1997: 76). However, would it be too inordinate to add a third sequence to this work ("Pärt's most minimalist"), a third sequence that seems to play such an important role in Pärt's 'second period'? Supplementing Hillier's analysis, I would suggest silence as the third major component of *Sarah* ..., traversing and combining the other two, withdrawing from them and at the same time nestling down into them: silence as a (divine) milieu.[11]

---

[9]   Concerning frugality, Pärt's music can be equated to many of Morton Feldman's works. Reflecting on his compositional process, Feldman writes that, in order to make a piece more interesting he begins taking away material rather than bringing more in: "What is needed in this piece? How much do I take out?" (Feldman 2000: 173).

[10]   *Sarah* ... somehow reminds me of Samuel Beckett's *Worstward Ho*: "On. Say on. Be said on. Somehow on. Till nohow on. Said nohow on .... Try again. Fail again. Fail better .... At bounds of boundless void. Whence no farther. Best worse no farther. Nohow less. Nohow worse. Nohow naught. Nohow on ... Said nohow on." No plot or narrative can be recognized. Nothing seems to be happening while innumerable things are happening. Ever-shifting configurations of some hundred words move frenetically back and forth, producing worlds of changing meanings and possibilities, a dense web of describable and ineffable relations and associations. Like Beckett's text, *Sarah* ... oscillates between a repetition of the non-identical and a variation of the same.

[11]   Of course, Hillier is aware of silence as a creative element in Pärt's music. In a chapter entitled 'Performance Practice' he writes that "so many of his works incorporate such frequent and sometimes extensive silences that they become thematic in effect and must be 'played'" (Hillier 1997: 199). However, Hillier is describing silence here as a function of the music, subordinated in the end, to the sounds; silence should be treated as music, as composed sounds. The idea I am presenting here proceeds from the opposite: Pärt's music is entirely at the service of silence. These silences escape any possible thematizing, and instead of trying to 'play' them, one should perhaps try 'not to play' the notated notes. In other words, the musicians cannot but violate the silence in order to make it appear as a non-thematic aspect of the work.

In the same chapter, Hillier specifically delineates a connection between silence and spirituality: "The *use* of silence in Pärt's music has been commented upon often enough,

In the sleeve-notes to the CD *Tabula Rasa*, Pärt takes down the outcome of his composing: "Everything that is unimportant falls away. Tintinnabulation is like this.[12] Here I am alone with silence. I have discovered that it is enough when a single note is beautifully played. This one note, or a silent beat, or a moment of silence, comforts me." The three compositions on this CD, *Fratres*, *Cantus*, and *Tabula Rasa*, are to some extent quite similar to *Sarah* .... Although *Sarah* ..., unlike the others, is not composed according to the tintinnabuli system, it already carries its traces. But more important here is the opportunity given, in all these works, to silence, an opportunity to let itself be heard.[13] By framing and containing it, the composed tones supply the silence with a context, giving it something to say, giving it a voice.

How appropriate the old title *Modus* here. *Modus/Sarah* ... is the way towards a boundary; it is composition taken to its limits, albeit in an affirmative way.

---

generally as contributing to a perception of the *music's spiritual nature*" (Hillier 1997: 199, my italics). What I am attempting to rethink in this chapter is the extent to which Pärt is actually 'using' silence, that is, the extent to which he is deliberately putting it into action and (thereby) controlling and ruling it. Secondly, in the process of writing this book I became less sure whether music can possess a 'spiritual nature.' Though many people tend to ascribe well-defined formalistic characteristics which they then associate with spirituality to music, I am not convinced that that is the best way to relate music and the spiritual because it too easily becomes quagmired in a process of in- and exclusion that is in the end rather aesthetical or political than philosophical.

[12]   Most of Pärt's pieces from 1976 on, starting with the tender piano solo *Für Alina* (Aliinale), are composed according to a principle known as tintinnabulation. According to the *OED*, tintinnabulum is a small tinkling bell. One could say that the form of many of Pärt's tintinnabuli compositions resembles the way in which a bell sounds. As Hillier writes,

   ... the tintinnabuli style is based on a simple system for relating the horizontal and vertical manifestations of pitch – melody and harmony (scales and arpeggiated triads) ... The characteristic sound of tintinnabuli music stems from a blend of diatonic scales and triadic arpeggios in which harmonic stasis is underpinned by the constant presence (actual or implied) of the tonic triad ... The basis of tintinnabuli style is a two-part texture (working always note against note), consisting of a 'melodic' voice moving mostly step by step from or towards a central pitch (often, but not always the tonic) and a 'tintinnabuli' voice sounding the notes of the tonic triad. (Hillier 1997: 90, 92–3)

[13]   *Tabula Rasa* is a slow piece for two violins, string orchestra and obbligato prepared piano in two movements: 'Ludus' (game, to play, to play music), marked 'con moto,' and 'Silentium' (silence, or action and contemplation), marked 'senza moto.' The work's first 'theme' is a single note, a *fortissimo* A on both solo violins, 4 octaves apart. ("The 'slate' is wiped clean," Hillier writes.) After this initial sound there follows a bar of silence, the work's second theme, according to Hillier. 'Ludus' is a game full of silences that grow progressively shorter until they are overwhelmed by a loud cadenza. 'Silentium' is slow and quiet. Though it has no actual silences until the very end, it can be regarded as a gradual preparation for silence, a slow unwinding into it (Hillier 1997: 114–15).

Both the percussive and vocal tones are brought to a place where they fall silent, to a place whereof they cannot testify. The sound of silence is a musical 'event horizon' where sound is directed away from audibility.[14]

The statement is sufficiently well-known: "Whereof one cannot speak, thereof must one be silent."[15] This sentence is certainly applicable to the relationship between language and music. The impossibilities of translating music into verbal language, to capture the meaning of music in words, to convert musical parameters to linguistic ones – these impossibilities are enlarged upon by so many thinkers on music; Vladimir Jankélévitch's book *Music and the Ineffable* is just one of the more appropriate examples. But doesn't Pärt's work bear witness to the supposition that this sentence number 7, the final one, from Ludwig Wittgenstein's *Tractatus Logico Philosophicus*, is also relevant for music itself, for music taken as a language? Can music be put to silence because it is not able to give evidence of ... of silence ... of the unnameable?[16]

In the beginning of *The Differend*, Lyotard distinguishes four different silences: the silence of the addressee (This case does not fall within your competence), the silence of the referent (This case does not exist), the silence of the sense (It cannot be signified), and the silence of the addressor (It does not fall within my competence). The differend – the neologism from which the book takes its title – is

> ... the unstable state and instant of language wherein something which must be able to be put into phrases cannot yet be. This state includes silence, which is a negative phrase, but it also calls upon phrases which are in principle possible. This state is signaled by what one ordinarily calls a feeling: 'One cannot find the words,' etc. (Lyotard 1988: 13)

In due course, words (music) can be found for what is felt in the silence of the differend; a new idiom, a new genre can be brought into existence. The impossibility is by nature factual, not principal. Transferred to music, this would suggest that it is only a matter of time before Pärt or another composer finds a way to express through music that which, until now, escapes it. This, however, is not the silence I am trying to thematize here; nor is it – at least in my opinion – the silence for which Pärt is making space. Later in his book,

---

[14]   The 'event horizon' is a term borrowed from astrophysics. It is the limit at which light is prohibited from streaming away from a black hole's gravitational pull.

[15]   The original German quote goes as follows: "Wovon man nicht sprechen kann, darüber muss man schweigen," also translated as "What we cannot speak about, we must pass over in silence" (Sentence no. 7 [the final sentence] of Wittgenstein's *Tractatus Logico Philosophicus*).

[16]   "Naming an object means suppressing three quarters of the play of a poem, which is made for guessing and suggesting, like a dream," writes Mallarmé, the poet of emptiness, whiteness, and silence (Mallarmé 1945: 869).

Lyotard introduces another silence, a fifth one, one that differs fundamentally from the four mentioned above. This fifth silence concerns presentation as such, or, rather, the possibility that a presentation becomes impossible:

> Which of the four kinds of silence is it? Or is this some other kind of silence? It is another kind of silence. One that does not bear upon an instance in a phrase universe, but which bears upon the occurrence of a phrase. There would be no more presentations. But you wrote: "For there to be no phrase is impossible"! That's just it: the feeling that the impossible is possible. That the necessary is contingent. That linkage must be made, but that there won't be anything upon which to link. The 'and' with nothing to grab onto. Hence, not just the contingency of the how of linking, but the vertigo of the last phrase. Absurd, of course. But the lightning flash takes place – it flashes and bursts out in the nothingness of the night, of the clouds, or of the clear blue sky. (Lyotard 1988: 75)

Sarah ... testifies of the impossible become possible. Here, silence is not a function of music, of sound, anymore, as in the more conventional use of pauses, fermatas, breaks, and the like; it has turned into a positive void rather than a negative one. The silences in *Sarah* ... are articulations of 'something' that escapes language, both linguistic and musical, though they can only be 'presented' through (musical) phrases, through the other-than-silence. Framed by music, they make the same music impossible: the silencing of sense and the becoming speechless of music.[17] It gives rise to the idea that only when we know how to be silent will that of which we cannot speak begin to tell us something.

Boom, boom, boom, tock ... Boom, boom, boom, tock ... Boom, boom, tock, boom ... Boom, boom, tock, boom ... Boom, tock, boom, boom ...

The rests after each sentence (here represented by the ellipsis) emphasize the impossibility of building larger, coherent phrases, able to drown out the silence. The music ebbs away for several seconds. The apex is not cached by some rich music; rather a contrapuntal play unfolds between the notated music (in all its discretion) and its surroundings.[18] *Sarah* ... is a hesitating play between presence and absence, an absence that can only be presented by a presence that negates this absence as absence. In other words, presence is needed in order to go 'beyond' it. It is brought to a limit in order to gain a provisional access to that which it tries to push aside. In order to write the erotic, the spiritual, in order to write experience, "I have been trying to talk a language that equals zero, a language

---

[17]   The same paradox can be found in a remark by Giya Kancheli, that other proclaimed representative of the New Spiritual Music movement, who feels himself related to medieval composers as they understood the concepts of silence and reflection so very well: "When you enter a church, synagogue, or mosque, there is a very specific silence. It is exactly this silence that I want to express in my music."

[18]   "Silence is my substitute for counterpoint," Morton Feldman remarks (Feldman 2000: 181).

equivalent to nothing at all, a language that returns to silence," Bataille notes in *Erotism* (Bataille 1986: 264).[19] Broken, jolting sentences, dotted lines, and empty pages are his tools to express his not-knowing, his speechlessness in the face of the sacred or the spiritual. Silence is the medium left for the composer of audible works to give voice to what cannot be expressed. Silence: for the composer the impalpable, the unmanipulatable, that to which he can give opportunity but which withdraws from his power and control. Admitting silence means accepting an element that relates asymmetrically to the human. Man and silence do not have a common measure; they are incommensurable. (In *Poetry, Language, Thought*, Heidegger notes that "the peal of stillness is not anything human" (1971: 207). Following Heidegger, one could say that such a peal or appeal rather abides in what one might call the other-than-human. However, in approaching a listener, a work has to betray the inhuman purity of silence.)[20] This incommensurability is quite audible: *vis-à-vis* the unpredictability of the silences, Pärt places composed segments, characterized by an utmost structuring, an almost mechanical and mathematical logic. The percussion part consists of a systematic displacement of the tom-tom with regard to the big drum as well as a predictable contraction technique. Following the second percussion part, the tenor voices make use of an easily discernable permutation technique, a technique that can also be recognized in the organ part immediately following the third percussion part – when the five two-part chords are played in different (however logical) orders according to the principle 1-2-3-4-5, 2-3-4-5-1, 3-4-5-1-2, and so on. In other words, the irregulable silences are surrounded by stringently ordered composed tones, almost contrary to the aural experience (see Ex. 10.3).

Pärt's carefully constructed music is searching for silence, searching for that which is beyond the sensual. His music is orbiting around silence, around an empty place, circling around 'something' that it can never reach or achieve and what music itself is not. *Sarah ...* is, to use the words of Walter Benjamin, a "song of an instant before disappearing into nothingness" (1972: 99), thereby creating an openness to otherness. Is that otherness a spiritual place, a place where a glimpse can be caught of something that might be called 'spiritual'? And is it here that spirituality can be experienced as a critical concept, an ever-receding horizon which our thinking and acting fails to reach?

---

[19] "And every time he does his work, makes something where there was nothing before, spoils that nice clean emptiness, he knows in some way that he's doing a bad thing," Daniel Stern writes in his novel *The Rose Rabbi*.

[20] Even the voices in *Sarah ...* somehow testify to the other-than-human. Bereft of lyrics, they announce the coming to pass of communication only in the act of its being given up, thrown back into secrecy. The work inclines toward a stranding of played and sung notes which leave human expression behind.

Example 10.3 'Sarah Was 90 Years Old', organ part 6 © 1991 by Universal
Edition A.G., Wien/UE 30300

Example 10.3 'Sarah Was 90 Years Old', organ part 6 (concluded) © 1991 by
Universal Edition A.G., Wien/UE 30300

In his biography on Pärt, Paul Hillier briefly mentions his compositional silence during the years 1968–76, characterized by a "searching out and stripping away of all that was alien," a process of purification during which Pärt becomes "highly sensitized to all noise" (Hillier 1997: 74). One could say that during this 'rite of passage,' Pärt is waiting and listening; he learns to wait and to listen, trying to conceive of a listening silence as an effort to give space to the inexpressible, thereby becoming Vasudeva.[21] Like Coltrane, Pärt learns that he is not in command, not ruling (anymore); rather he is receiving and subservient to the musical material. His compositional attitude could be described as a making space for the musical event, preparing a space where the event can happen. This is what Lyotard in *The Inhuman* calls *passibility*, somewhat commensurate to Heidegger's *sein-lassen*, letting be. This does not imply an indifference of man towards beings (everything that 'is'), to let beings take their course without involvement. On the contrary. *Sein-lassen* is much more than simply respect and worship for beings. However, it is not a human activity or action in the usual sense. *Sein-lassen* is creating a space where beings can be, where beings can prosper, kindle, come. *Sein-lassen* is *andenkend Denken.*[22] In much the same way – explicitly referring to Heidegger's *Ereignis*, an event or occurrence that can only be approached through a state of privation – Lyotard writes in *L'inhumain* [*The Inhuman*]:

> Thinking, like writing or painting [or composing], is almost no more than letting a givable come towards you. ... In what we call thinking the mind isn't 'directed' but suspended. You don't give it rules. You teach it to receive. You don't clear the ground to build unobstructed: you make a little clearing where the penumbra of an almost-given will be able to enter and modify its contour. (Lyotard 1991: 18–19)

A clearing (Heidegger's *Lichtung*) is created; a place is laid bare where the unpresentable is unconcealed in its concealedness, presented in its absence, a place where the unnameable is introduced. However, this can only have a chance of success if thought itself resolves to be irresolute, decides to be patient, wanting not to want, wanting, precisely, not to produce a meaning in place of giving voice to what *must* be signified.[23]

---

[21] "This was among the ferryman's virtues one of the greatest: like only a few, he knew how to listen. Without him having spoken a word, the speaker sensed how Vasudeva let his words enter his mind, quiet, open, waiting, how he did not lose a single one, awaited not a single one with impatience, did not add his praise or rebuke, was just listening," writes Hermann Hesse in *Siddhartha* (Hesse 1960: 98).

[22] See, for example, Heidegger's *Letter on Humanism* (1946). See also Threshold 7.

[23] Waiting and listening, being patient and responsive: these are the words with which Morton Feldman too describes his work as a composer. "Sometimes a day's working is waiting ... I clean my *teppich*, read books on *teppich*, I clean the house, always waiting" (Feldman 2000: 163). Waiting to reach the right level of concentration in which music that escapes from the supremacy of the narrative Self can be produced or can produce itself. Paraphrasing the old proverb "Man makes plans, God laughs," Feldman writes: "The composer makes plans, music laughs" in order to emphasize that it is not he who creates

Pärt gives silence a space – a silence that can be called, using the words of Lyotard, an 'immaterial materiality'– though this giving space can only find its occasion at the cost of suspending the active powers of the mind, a possibility in which the mind is accessible but not prepared for the (material) event of silence to occur (Lyotard 1991: 140).

To give silence a space, to give silence something to say; this should not be regarded as something which Pärt consciously 'evokes' in his works. Although it is Pärt who is acting, composing, introducing a certain order, it is not Pärt who is speaking here or using his works as a means to 'show' something. Possibility alludes to the restraint of the composer.[24] Pärt is not a composer in the ordinary sense; his composing attitude is marked by the will not to want, the intention not to intend: where there is *no* will, there is a way. His work (*Sarah ...*) is not his 'work' but a *sein-lassen*, the creating of a space where a composition can happen. This does not imply that Pärt's composing is absolutely unpredictable or irrational or that it happens coincidentally. It is not without form; on the contrary, it demands efforts, skills, and concentration.[25] The composition is constructed with great care and is almost predictable in its formal structure. The paradox is that the indeterminate can only appear through deliberate methods. Mastery and expertise play their part, but also of utmost importance is a moment of surrender that cannot be planned.[26]

"The music that is beautiful to me, *dis-covers itself,* emerges from silence, from being silent. When I am silent for a longer period, music comes into being,"

'his' music; it is already there, and he has a conversation with the material. "I listen to my sounds, and I do what they tell me, not what I tell them. Because I owe my life to these sounds" (Feldman 2000: 111). For Feldman, everything is a found object. Everything he does feels essentially not his, not belonging to him. "The question continually on my mind all these years is: to what degree does one give up control, and still keep that last vestige where one can call the work one's own? Everyone must find his own answer here" (Feldman 2000: 30).

[24]   Mostly contemplating the silent music of Scelsi, Feldman, and Nono, Peter Niklas Wilson speaks in *Musik und Religion* of a reduction of the musical material to a few, essential elements, a process requiring a concentration on the quality of single tones or simple intervals and in which the composing subject withdraws in order to let the sounds be themselves (Wilson 1995: 331).

[25]   At the edge of being silent, when routine fails, significant compositional problems are not easy to solve, notices Theo Hirsbrunner in his monograph (2003) on Claude Debussy.

[26]   These thoughts on Pärt's compositional possibility also apply, *mutatis mutandis*, to the performer and listener of his music. Dealing with these fragile sounds, one should not attempt to be virtuoso, because that will not match the fostered austerity of the music. However, as Hillier writes, "it takes a gifted performer to meet the challenge of playing the notes in a way that does not do violence to the music's essential serenity" (Hillier 1997: 106). In addition, listening to this silent music is not only an aesthetical act but a ritual exercising as well, an initiation ceremony, as Peter Niklas Wilson (1995) remarks (with some implied disgust).

Pärt says during an interview.[27] His possibility not only allows music to arise from silence; it also allows it to return to silence. And this should not be understood solely in a linear, sequential manner: it is already *in* the desolate(d) tones with which *Sarah* ... is composed that silence becomes experienceable, 'audible.' The notated sounds already testify to an ungraspable silence.[28] Pärt yields the music back to silence.[29]

Relating silence and spirituality is, of course, not new. Whereas the Logos of Christian epistemology principally links spiritual knowledge to language – "The Word is become flesh" – the older Greco-Roman tradition departs in the direction of an unknown god who silences all thought because he is without being. In the Plotinian ontology of the One, language is excluded from spiritual experience. In the sixteenth century, Western mystics reintroduce into the Christian discourse something of this Greek silence of the past. In that respect, the mystic phrase is an artifact of silence, trying to produce silence in the murmur of words (De Certeau 1992: 115 and 150).[30]

However, this tradition may come somewhat too close to a negative theology, as the assumption of Plotinian and mystic Christian One-ness still presupposes a presence, albeit one that cannot be (re)presented in language. The silences of *Sarah* ... are maybe less reassuring, less confident of the existence of a comprehensive and ubiquitous Presence; perhaps they are (thus) all the more threatening because they are surrounded by that warm bath of slow, modal, static sounds.

In the beginning of his book on Pärt, Paul Hillier writes:

> An encounter with 'silence' brings us not only to the mystical tradition, in which silence is at once profound and positive, but close also to the modern fear of silence as absence: the silence of a God who is otherwise engaged, or simply not there. From the one point of view, silence is filled with an apprehension of presence and compassion, while from the other it presents us with a sense of utter aloneness. (Hillier 1997: 10)

the modern 'fear' of silence

---

[27]   Pärt, in conversation with Horst Schwemmer, Vienna, March 15, 1981 (my italics).

[28]   Paradoxically, one of the elements that induces the hearing of silence in *Sarah* ... is the echo present throughout the whole work. So, it is in fact the permanent absence of silence due to the resonances of percussion and voices that evokes the experience of (almost complete) silence, of retraction, of emptiness.

[29]   "All music emerges from silence, to which sooner or later it must return," is the opening sentence of Hillier's book on Pärt, the first sentence in a paragraph entitled 'Music and Spirituality' (Hillier 1997: 1). It is probably not surprising that this sentence brings to mind Genesis 3:19: "[...] you return to the ground, since from it you were taken; for dust you are and to dust you will return."

[30]   "Oh, you who are curious to know what it is like to enjoy the Word, do not lend it your ear but your spirit. It is grace that teaches it, not language," mystic Diego de Jesus (1570–1621) writes in *Apuntamientos*, a treatise dealing with "lofty and spiritual" matters in which "grace rather than language is mistress."

The question is whether the silence that Hillier relates to the mystical tradition, a positive and profound silence, must indeed be opposed to a thereby non-mystical silence, filled with fear and absence. In other words, how 'positive' and 'compassionate' is or was this mystical tradition? In a short essay on the state and position of the sacred in the twentieth century, Georges Bataille states that spirituality has died of languishment and listless destitution. Following his diagnosis, ideas on spirituality have experienced a decrease because they became too pure, not frightening enough. (What needs to be remembered in this respect is that not only God is sacred for the Church, the Devil is as well, and it is exactly the fear animated by the Devil that counteracts the decrease.) It is the dismay that incites the sense for the spiritual, a sense that is dying in the presence of contemporary man's feebleness, as he does not realize anymore that nothing fascinates more than dismay. Bataille is adamant here: as long as we only long for security and ease, we will never possess the sense for the spiritual (Bataille 1970: 187–9). Bataille's atheology is based on the subversive effect and meaning of the sacred, that is, the boundaries of instrumentality and livable life. His reflection on the absence of God (negative) immediately transforms into a reflection on God-as-absence (positive).

Is not the spiritual Presence and compassion, articulated (according to Hillier) in a positive silence, a twentieth-century invention, approaching the Glad Tidings of some New Age gurus? If we take the analyses and meditations of people like Bataille, De Certeau, Taylor (and many others who leave their traces in this book) seriously, spirituality (and silence in its wake) is not a concept referring to an unproblematic contact with God, a Self (already more secularized), nor any other transcendental signified. The silence advanced here is "the silence of the hysteric" (Lyotard 1984b: 102).[31]

Boom, boom, boom, tock … Boom, boom, boom, tock … Boom, boom, tock, boom … Boom, boom, tock, boom … Boom, tock, boom, boom …

---

[31] Lyotard opposes the silence of the hysteric to the analyst's silence (the pure silence of ratio). He recognizes two silences with inverse functions: the silence of noise, of the imaginary, and the silence of structure, of the symbolical. According to Lyotard the latter, the silence of the Signifier, the silence of order and composition, attempts to dissipate the former silence, the noise-silence, the silence that escapes from every order and unification.

What is needed is a 'practice' (a word probably devoid of meaning as soon as it no longer refers to a 'subject'), a practice that is not dominated, without domain, without domus, without the cupola of the Duomo of Florence in Brunelleschi's little box, but also the vessel of the Ark of the Covenant that contains the stone tablets. Without arche: and even without an-arche. (Lyotard 1984b: 102–9)

The empty tones surrounding silence and simultaneously surrounded by it, give little grip for the listener. He is thrown upon his own resources. What remains is the possibility of a naked, (un)responsive listening, deprived of a clear frame. Listening becomes a ceremony, a ritual, instead of a merely aesthetical affair. Through listening, the relationship between music and spirituality takes place.

THRESHOLD 11
Listening to Music

ONE conviction which I have tried to articulate so far is that there is no specific music that can bring us into contact with the spiritual. There are no intrinsic qualities which would legitimize ascribing the adjective 'spiritual' to the noun 'music.' It is difficult, if not impossible, to compile the characteristics or parameters that would ensure the spiritual dimensions of certain music. In *Modern Music and After*, Paul Griffiths asks himself rhetorically

> ... whether music can be divided at all into the spiritual and the non-spiritual, or whether spirituality does not rather reside in the music's texts (Pärt and Tavener, for instance, have set almost exclusively sacred texts, often in sacred languages) and – most of all – in *how the music is heard*. (Griffiths 1995: 276, my italics)[1]

What takes place here is a shift from regarding spirituality as an objective condition towards understanding it as a relationship between a subject and an object, which could be called 'spiritual':[2] not spiritual music, but a connection between two vibrating bodies, the sound producer and the sound receiver, described discursively as 'spiritual.' With this shift, the distinction between profane and spiritual music can, as a last resort, be traced back to the way music is listened to, and, subsequently, how this listening experience is articulated in language.[3]

---

[1]   I leave behind here the traditional tripartition composer–interpreter–listener. Instead, I regard the composer as the initial listener to his own work and the act of interpreting as an activity based upon the ability to listen.

[2]   An analogous argument is presented by Nicolas Cook when he states that musical meaning is constructed through the music – interpreter interaction. It is wrong, he writes, to speak of music *having* particular meanings (Cook 2001: 180).

[3]   Even Joscelyn Godwin, who is so keen on proving the spiritual dimension of music (see Threshold 5), admits to the crucial role of the listener:

> It is the listener who now becomes an indispensable participant, and whose activity is perhaps the main goal, rather than the expression of the composer's emotions or of the performer's virtuosity. We may have seen the end of the epoch of Great Composers, which will after all only have lasted about 500 years. Music can do without them, as it does almost everywhere else in the world. The listener or singer can reach the ultimate states that music can offer just as well through plainchant or folk music as through the grandiose apparatus of Bayreuth or the Ninth Symphony. The new emphasis on the listener and on the act of listening invites everyone without exception to participate in music to the utmost, just as the outpouring of formerly guarded knowledge enables individuals to pursue their spiritual quests independently of church dogmas and authority. (Godwin 1987: 122)

Locating the decisive moment within the act of hearing, however, also implies the possibility that the listener will not recognize the spiritual, although this can never be retraced completely to free choice: the cultural, political, and religious organizational structures of a society (including their discourses) play important roles here.

The foregoing brings us to the question as to how listening can establish a contact between sound source and receiver that might be adorned with the term 'spiritual' as set forth in the previous thresholds. In other words, how to understand, how to define this listening attitude, this necessary link to connect music and spirituality?

In a television interview, Pierre Boulez mentions a writer who once said that music is at first a mystery, then, after studying it, everything becomes clear, and, finally, with the performance, it becomes a mystery once again.[4] This writer recognizes an experience after or on the other side of analysis, that is, beyond the constituting syntheses of an analyzing subject. With this, he goes beyond the famous listening theory and typology of Theodor Wiesengrund Adorno. In the opening essay of *The Introduction to the Sociology of Music* (1976) entitled 'Types of Musical Conduct,' Adorno champions a 'structural listening,' an entirely adequate hearing that makes it possible to understand the structural components and internal logic of even the most complicated music. The listener should focus on the formal relationships within the music and in so doing try to comprehend them, that is, make them meaningful through the process of reflection. The execution of this 'high art of listening' relies principally on the application of skills acquired in a music-technical education and is, according to Adorno, reserved almost exclusively for professional musicians:[5] the only person who can solve the riddle of music is the one who plays it correctly (Leppert 2002: 139).[6]

I would like to comment on Adorno's theory and typology of listeners because it is still so influential in the development of theories concerning listening to music.

---

[4]   I must confess that I can recall the memory but not the exact reference.

[5]   Adorno's plea reminds me of that of the nineteenth-century German music theorist Georg Gottfried Gervinus who in 1868 wrote that "every instrumental work has every claim on every kind of respect, provided that it is addressed exclusively to the only audience deserving of it, namely the *cognoscenti* – those who know and are in a position to judge its formal worth" (quoted in Goehr 1994: 237). Gervinus, however, uses the argument in a society and an era which was on its way to stilling a music audience accustomed to dancing, conversing, applauding, chattering, and singing along with a performance. Musical performances tended to be more affairs in the background, providing a good occasion for socializing. Music definitely was not listened to or esteemed of itself. After 1800 the climate changed. Audiences were asked to be silent, so that the work, its beauty (and even its truth), could be heard in and of itself (Goehr 1994: 192–3 and 236–40).

[6]   Adorno's structural listening completely ignores anything external to the compositional structure; the name of the composer or the composition, for example, is deemed not important at all. A work obscured behind its name, behind the name of the one who composed it, or behind the names of some famous performers, might only be heard as an experience of its fame. Music, however, should be engaged with on its own terms.

Structural listening implies also a criticism of so-called 'atomistic listening' where an experience of the musical process becomes lost in the catching of some thematic snippets. "The right way to hear music includes a spontaneous awareness of the non-identity of the whole and the parts as well as the synthesis that unites the two," Adorno writes in 'Little Heresy' (Leppert 2002: 321).

First, Adorno's preferred listening attitude, requiring so much musical education, theoretical training, and specialized knowledge, is related directly to a penchant for a specific kind of music, that is, Western art music after 1800, in which improvisation is gradually excluded and a fixed musical structure with unchangeable internal components and relationships becomes the new standard. In other words, Adorno's warm recommendations are in fact not rooted in some universal conditions on listening but in particular historical circumstances and his own specific cultural predilections.[7]

In other words, how 'applicable' are Adorno's ideas on structural listening with regard to other music, to certain contemporary electronic music for example, to music often vaguely referred to as *glitch*, to the music of Ryoji Ikeda, Alva Noto, and Pan Sonic?[8]

Second, presupposed in this typology is an autonomous subject, the modern subject of the Enlightenment (see also Threshold 6). Adorno's ideological framework is marked by a confidence in the constituting syntheses of the listening subject, who is able to contemplate music from a certain (scientifically informed) distance. Only through the subjective synthesis does music receive its significance, become a whole, and is as a whole transparent for understanding.

Third (and following from the second remark), alongside this idea of *clairaudience*, Adorno passes over or, better, does not move further into the third phase of Boulez's writer, the 'mysterious' experience of what announces itself after, beyond, or through a profound analysis. Although quantitatively hardly worth noting, the leading position in Adorno's listeners' typology is occupied by the expert, relying on his rationality and knowledge of concrete musical logic. Some questions remaining are if other approaches to listening are possible, if structural listening is indeed the highest aim, and if it is the ultimate position upon which the listener can recline, coddled by his own knowledge.

---

[7] Rose Subotnik uses this argument in her essay 'Towards a Deconstruction of Structural Listening' in *Deconstructive Variations* (Subotnik 1996: 157–8).

[8] The word glitch is derived from the Yiddish 'glitshn': to slip, slide, or glide. Something glitchy is slippery and out of control. Glitch is a minor malfunction or spurious signal, often related to a digital system or an electronic device. It is commonly used to describe errors in computer software or hardware, the crashing of computers, or the sound of a CD or sound file skipping and stuttering. It is not a collapse of the machinery. The machinery is still running, but the performance is poor – either annoying, problematic or downright useless.

Glitch music incorporates these and related sounds. Apart from damaging CDs, glitch artists collapse software processing, for example by overloading processors, reducing bit rates or reading files from another file format (text files, picture files, program files) as if they were audio files. The results are sampled and inserted into a musical context.

In the rest of this chapter I focus especially on the subgenre *Minimal Click*: dry, repetitive movements of the tiniest, sometimes barely audible, clicks of computer and sound technology. These sounds are exposed musically, often without adding melodic material that would stifle the fragile clicks (Sangild 2004: 258–60).

It is, however, not my intention to promptly disregard and surpass Adorno's ideas on structural listening here, offering in exchange ideas about a relationship with music that could be marked by the term 'spiritual.' Though this entirely adequate hearing seems to assume a subject who surveys and relies on rational knowledge, it also postulates a deep respect for music; one might perhaps even call it surrender. Adorno makes clear that for a work to be fully realized, the act of reception must somehow meet the music's immanent demands. Music as a product of human labor places demands on the receiver, to the extent that it exists not merely for easy consumption – designated with the term 'regressive listening' – but because it has something to say. The reception of music should involve an act of cognition and an act of respect and responsibility – not only because one is listening to music but also because one is receiving the product of another human being who, through art, is attempting to speak. Adorno seems to require both an active and a passive attitude from the listener. The susceptibility or receptivity that Adorno has in mind is passive, passive in its dedication to the music which unfolds itself. Yet, a certain preparation is necessary. The music also demands the intelligent and active participation of the listener. A composition can only be understood in the passing through of it, following its course with total, active, and constructive attention. The active role of the listener offers as a corollary an opening up of meaningfulness that comes into existence through the relation *between* the work and the listener. In other words, one deduction which can be derived from Adorno's thoughts is that it requires a listener at least to discover or to create meaning in music (spiritual meaning, for example), which implies that 'everything' in fact germinates from the relation between the music and its audience.

This attentive listening, however, is not sufficient in order to gain a clearer insight into what announces itself beyond the subject-with-and-for-itself of which Boulez's writer speaks. In order to make space for a listening experience that is not (only) predetermined by an analytical attitude, it is necessary to relinquish Adorno's ideas on structural listening.[9] For, before or beyond an intentional, signifying, and cognitive listening, an other listening can be traced, a listening not immediately intended for the benefit of rationality, understanding, and logic. Besides becoming the indication of a concept, category, or theory, music is also "an event which grips my body," that enters my body, that solicits my body's participation, regardless of what may or may not be my own (intentional) interests, judgments, and desires (Merleau-Ponty 1962: 235). "Is it the plot or the sensuous moment that draws us back again and again to the same music?" asks Rose Subotnik rhetorically in her analysis and deconstruction of Adorno's ideas on structural listening. And she continues: "Music always confronts us with the actuality of a medium that remains stubbornly resistant to strategies of abstract reduction" (Subotnik 1996: 174–6).

---

[9]   This paragraph is based primarily on two essays by Geraldine Finn, 'Giving Place – Making Space – For Truth – In Music' and 'To Speculate – On Music – and/as the Sound of *Différance*' (Finn 2002: 189–95).

It is first of all the sounding of music – the acoustical and not the grammatical component – that is infectious; not the intentionality of its organization (its system, structure or sense) which names, frames and contains it as sonata or rondo, as tonal or atonal, as F minor or B♭, as popular or classical music but affection.[10] The acoustical component gives the grammatical (signifying, structural, semantic) component effectivity, agency and force, by a direct access to the body. Besides, it provides access to traces of a space between, a space between categories, concepts, and words. It makes them almost trivial, though not completely superfluous. For the grammatical component confers legitimacy, authority, and direction on what we hear in or from this space between. It turns the sound of music into a sign and gives some (intelligible) direction to the corporeal infection of the sounds. However, the sense of sound is never secure(d). The force of the corporeal and the sensory always exceeds the cognitive structures of signification that claim and aim to name and contain it, just as data always resists the coherency of the image which we are trying to fashion of them.[11]

Listening constantly moves or operates between the grammatical and the acoustical, between the semantic and the corporeal, between concept and vibration. It cannot be reduced to the one or the other. In this respect, Adorno's theory on structural listening contains shortcomings; it is too one-sided. Listening also involves an opening of the senses that is not necessarily enfolded in conscious meaningfulness, by sense. It also takes place outside, before or beyond sense; it also refers to a sense that operates outside, before or beyond signification.[12]

---

[10]   Especially in his later works, Italian composer Luigi Nono strived to compose music that calls for a listening stance in which comprehension is not the aim. Rather, he wanted his music to be listened to in a non-interpretative manner, that is listening to the sounds 'themselves' instead of listening for what the sounds refer to, listening to sounds without trying to assign any kind of meaning to them other than how they appear in space and time.

[11]   Following Lacan, David Schwarz distinguishes in his book *Listening Subjects* between 'listening as a thing' and 'listening as a space.' The former concentrates on the analysis of music from a stable perspective, formalistic and transhistorical, a description of the musical structure and its internal relations. The latter is produced when "musical-theoretical, musical-historical, cultural, psychoanalytic, or personal thresholds are crossed and enunciated," thereby opening a fundamentally heterogeneous and fragmented listening experience (Schwarz 1997: 3–4 and 85). In a way, one could say that the slit in the work of Adorno becomes a gaping hole in Lacan's psycho-analytically oriented philosophy, in which the listener's subjective position is created through a complex intermingling of different discourses.

[12]   It is definitely not my intention to create a new dichotomy here – sensuous recognition versus conceptual interpretation. Rather, I would say that the one is always already present in the other. The sensuous can never be entirely absent, even in the most formal analyses. And structured understanding is never totally lacking even in what seems to be overtly sensuous presentations. It is a false assumption that these two modes of listening are mutually exclusive. How can making sense take place without the senses? And how can sensory experience not make sense? There are just different phases of

In *À l'écoute* [*Listening*] – meaning both 'to be listening' and 'to be receptive' – French thinker Jean-Luc Nancy describes this as 'l'écoute de l'outre-sens.' Listening does not immediately appeal to understanding, sense, meaning, signification; it (also) makes an encounter possible with the not-yet-coded, the non-coded, and perhaps even the de-coded, in short, an encounter with what is outside meaning or beyond comprehension (Nancy 2002: 60 and 69).[13] (It is due to the fundamental difference between the sonorous and the logical – the *logos* – that causes Nancy to wonder if philosophy will ever be capable of listening.) Or perhaps it is better to say that to be listening, to be listening to music, always means to be at the edge of meaning, as music's meaning is to be found in the sonorous or in the resonance itself (which implies that music is always already more than a purely acoustic phenomenon).[14] Music is situated in the space between sense and sound, between theory and resonance. However, sense and sound are not (only) opposed. There is also a sense of or in sound. Part of music's meaning encountered in a listening or corporeal experience is of an other order than the order of thinking and naming, which places the meaning of music outside of the music; it is situated precisely in the materiality of the music, in its rhythm and timbre. Therefore Nancy writes that musical sense is syntactical without being semantic, communicating the incommunicable, communicating nothing but itself (Nancy 2002: 79).

Actually, Nancy states, the possibility to attribute meaning to a sonorous event, to music, through listening, can only take place because this possibility is itself incorporated in or made possible by 'something' else, something that thus precedes this possibility, described by Nancy as 'the resonance of sound.' Meaning (if there is one) is never neutral, colorless, or voiceless; it comes into being thanks to or by means of the sonorous material of the music (which is, first of all, rhythm and timbre). Music is not only language minus meaning, as Claude Lévi-Strauss asserts; parallel to this idea, music can also be regarded as meaning without language.

On the other side of structural listening, beyond attributing sense and (transcendental) signification to music, before (and after) explication and

---

listening, of encountering and understanding music. What is needed is a recognition of continuity between these phases. (See, for a more elaborate meditation on this subject, Cumming [2000].)

[13]   Nancy's ideas bear some resemblance to Heidegger's. The latter asks us not to listen (solely) to formulas and formulations but first and foremost to the *Grundton* or timbre of a text or phrase. Heidegger is referring here to 'the other' of saying, an unruly rest that is also the precondition for every saying; instead of stressing a logical-discursive approach, he demands attention for what resonates, what (re)sounds. However, as Heidegger is hardly addressing music (unlike Nancy), one could ask the question as to what extent his use of words like *Grundton* remains limited to a metaphorical usage.

[14]   In the strict sense, music can never be called a phenomenon as it does not meet the logic of a manifestation. That is why Nancy opts instead for the word 'evocation.'

comprehension, there is a possible encounter with music that I would call spiritual.[15] Listening to music beyond or before its categorical frameworks is a spiritual experience, a coming across a space between, a passage beyond the synthesizing ego (the 'I' is not a *fundamentum inconcussum* but a *medium percussum*, Peter Sloterdijk [1993] writes) and its objects – structural listening and the objectified musical work. This spirituality, however, has nothing to do with immateriality; it takes us right down to the material, to 'the real' of music, to the mysteries of the existence of material beings as material beings, to the excess of being over thought, that is, over a spirituality that resorts to transcendental signifiers like God, Oneness or Soul. Spirituality in reference to music means experiencing the materiality of music outside or beyond its linguistically constructed borders.

In the above, I briefly mentioned *glitch* as an example of contemporary electronic music which would be difficult to approach through structural listening. The sense of this music, and especially its subgenre *Minimal Click*, can most likely only be found in its sonorous material, in its timbre and rhythm. To try to analyze this music in terms of melodic and/or harmonic developments is simply inadequate and perhaps even impossible. *Minimal Click* focuses on frail and fragile sounds, scarcely audible in normal situations or unnoticed as marginal sounds of electronic equipment. Withdrawn from their customary environment, stripped from their preexisting significations, and inserted into a new sound space, they are endowed with a relative autonomy and thereby can conceivably be perceived as music. The Japanese composer Ryoji Ikeda is an important representative of this movement. For example, the title track on his album +/- consists solely of ultrasounds.[16] Torben Sangild correctly argues that with normal or poor speakers one almost doesn't hear anything until the track stops and a sudden release of tension is perceived: "what you hear is the sound ending, not its presence" (Sangild 2004: 265). According to Sangild '+/-' draws attention to the stress of unnoticed sounds in technological environments. With this last remark he draws what seems to be a logical parallel between sounds going unheard and going unnoticed. After all, our most recognized (bodily) site for making contact with sounds is the auditory organ. However, how strange would it be to explore the idea that listening exceeds the auditory organ? In *More Brilliant Than The Sun* 'concept engineer' Kodwo Eshun develops this thought, writing mainly about dance music as being simultaneously a kinaesthetic and a headmusic, a constant interaction between the sonic and the sensory.

---

[15] This encounter could be called immediate though this should not be regarded as an immediacy preceding reflection; rather, this immediacy appears after or through the (self)reflexivity of the conscious perception.

[16] Ultrasounds are frequencies above normal human hearing ability, conventionally over 20,000 hertz. Some animals hear them clearly: bats for instance use them to navigate. Humans use ultrasounds to explore flaws and defects in solid material. At high intensity, ultrasounds can be extremely stressful to living organisms and can be used to kill insects.

Whenever in Drum 'n' Bass the sound gets very scratchy, with lots of shakers and rattlers, there's often a lot of sounds where the percussion is too distributed, too motile and too mobile for the ear to grasp as a solid sound. And once the ear stops grasping this as solid sound, the sound very quickly travels to the skin instead – and the skin starts to hear for you. The skin starts to feel what the ears cannot. And whenever the skin starts to hear, that's where you feel all creepy crawly, and that's when conduction creeps in, when people say, 'I felt really cold', or that the music is really cold: which is because their skin has dropped maybe a centigrade as the music has hit it, as the beat has pressed across it." (Eshun 1998: 181)

The music Eshun is talking about – most often produced and transmitted by means of new technologies – is getting subdermal. It is the skin that hears: dermal ears. The sounds become a tactile sensation that *sussurates* the body, communicating paralinguistically with one's sensory system.[17]

I agree with Eshun that new technologies – at least regarding the ways in which they are used to make music – do not at all lead to the well-known elaborations on what is called the virtualization of the body or the disembodiment of the human. On the contrary, the computers used in *Minimal Click*, the turntables and rhythm machines in Rap, the techniques of scratching and sampling in Hip-Hop – all this makes listeners *feel* more intensely, all this leads to a renewed but also transformed contact with the senses: the feet that move, the hips that sway, the arms that swing, the head that nods, the nerves that pulse, the blood that pumps, the ears that register: it is the whole body that counts, it is the whole body that listens to music.[18]

Starting from a phenomenological point of view, Nancy comes to approximately the same conclusion when he discerns two vibrating bodies, one being the sound source, the other the body of the listener. Both bodies are vibrating and resonating, that is, extending, becoming and resolving in vibrations that simultaneously take them back to themselves and outside of themselves.[19] Vibration is a motion of infinite transmission and returning, a dynamics of coming and going, and therefore essentially mobile. And when this is a characteristic of both the sound emitter

---

[17]   Rapper Craig Mack says it this way: "When kinetic sensations organized into art are transmitted through a single sensory channel, through this single channel they can convey all the other senses at once, rhythmic, dynamic, tactile and kinetic sensations that make use of both the auditory and visual channels" (cited in Eshun 1998: 72).

[18]   It should be noted that a listening body is always already a sounding body as well. The sonorous activities comprise all somatic places – the rhythmic pulsation of the heart, the contraction or relaxation of the muscles, the amplification of the respiration, the shivers of the epidermis, not to forget the so-called otoacoustic emissions, sounds produced by the internal ear of the listener that mix with the external ones (Nancy 2002: 36 and 55). It reminds me of Stockhausen's comment that there consists a whole system of periodic rhythms within the body, from very fast to very slow ones. And together, all of these build a very polymeric music in the body.

[19]   It is the 're' in resonating that is important here. Vibrating is always already *re*-vibrating, going back and forth, emitting and returning, extension and penetration.

and sound receiver, to listen means to penetrate as well as to be penetrated, to be connected to the outside as well as the inside, to be passive (in receiving) as well as active (in giving back), to be (a vibrating body) as well as not to be (a proper and stable self, fully present to itself). Just like sounding, listening *is* resonating, moving back and forth, that is, taking place in a space between here and there, between self and other, between what occurs in the body and outside of it, in the space between two vibrating bodies; a vibrating body *is* only in relation.[20]

Listening *to* music means listening *to and fro* music. To experience this movement, this dynamic coming and going, means to experience it beyond those who are in this space, the listening subject and the sounding object. The intertwining is not simply the collection of subject and object, nor is it a function of these two. It is the interval between them, and this interval is irreducible to its components: to listen to and fro decenters them, wipes them out.

Would it be possible to call this the spiritual power of listening (to music), the spiritual power which enables man to lose himself or go beyond himself because subjectivity turns out to be medial instead of fundamental in nature? It is (partly) through the encounter with music that Sufism teaches the deconstruction of the opposition between subject and object and the opening of an entrance to the spiritual (see Threshold 5). However, disposed of its otherworldly overtones, it is through a phenomenological approach to listening – listening regarded as vibration and as a bodily experience – that another possibility announces itself, a possibility to encounter another other world, a world on this side that nevertheless

---

[20] Experiencing the vibrating body thus leads to a destabilization of the self as an autonomous subject; the 'well-definable unity conscious to itself' is criticized by rethinking what it means to listen. This idea is replaced by the thought that subjects are always already formed in and through interactions, which implies that they are formed through difference: a (temporary) 'self' only comes into existence through 'others.' These (social) processes of identity formation lead to a radically decentered 'self,' decentered by the idea of the intertwining of self and other: a differential interplay, an interplay of identity and difference.

Naturally following from this line of argument, redefining listening leads to an idea of the body as grounded in a non-dualistic intercorporeality, as a chiasmic openness to others; no fusion of subject and object but also no ontological divide. As for the object, this implies that the constitution of the other does not come after that of the body; others and body are born together. Regarding the subject, one could conclude that the 'self' is open to processes of change and should be defined in terms of the dynamics of change and growth.

Rethinking the self through listening means that, when I hear myself, when I listen to myself, to my words as well as to the sounds my voice makes, I can hear others: I can hear others 'inside' myself. Living others, dead others, others nearby and others far off. But the reverse is also true. When I listen to the other, I can hear myself; I hear myself 'in' or 'through' others, in and through music. The listener exists within the music, is seduced, captivated, and alienated by it. Listening thus refers to a space between the listener and the music, between self and other, or, better, going to and fro self and other (Levin 1989: 182 and 272). Regarded this way, listening – active listening – can claim to transcend the dualism implicit in most hermeneutical enterprises.

cannot be reduced to the knowable, the nameable, the frameable, the locatable, the familiar, and so on. Deconstructing the opposition between subject and object through listening might be considered as one aspect of listening's spiritual power. Listening introduces us to the unfamiliar, the unfamiliar in our thinking.

In Western philosophy, both Heidegger and Gadamer explicitly attribute a more fundamental openness to listening than to questioning because the way in which a question is posed limits and conditions the quality and level of any answer that might possibly be worked out: questioning is still too *logocratic*.[21] (Isn't questioning very often the main part of praying?) Listening, true listening, is different from the sort of cognitive endeavors that result in further production of the very knowledge that warrants them; it is 'the de-stitution of the defining' (Fiumara 1990: 21). In *Wahrheit und Methode* [*Truth and Method*], Gadamer states that "anyone who listens is fundamentally open. Without this kind of openness to one another there is no genuine human relationship. Belonging together always also means being able to listen to one another" (Gadamer 1979: 324). That any real listener is fundamentally open attunes to Heidegger's idea about the most basic condition of our being-in-the-world, an *ek-stasis*, an opening openness that connects us to Being as a whole. In *Sein und Zeit* [*Being and Time*] he writes that "being with others develops in listening to one another" (Heidegger 1962: 206).[22]

Gemma Corradi Fiumara's analyses of our Western culture, however, show that we have somehow lost this open(ing) attitude: we know how to speak, but not how to listen. In *The Other Side of Language* (1990) Fiumara chiefly blames logocentrism – and with that, its rationality, logic, and the need for ordering and systematization – in which speech is superior to listening and in which rational and technocratic discourses try to silence every deviating voice which might create links that are regarded as unnecessary. Institutional and discursive frameworks deafen what Fiumara calls 'the incessant rumbling of our cultural world.' Through speech we build ourselves a world of rational, coherent, and logical systems, a ruling set of meanings that appear to control and shape all of our rational pursuits; at the same time we reduce the silent, listening other to a void, a negation. Fiumara speaks of an increasingly arrogant logos, constituting itself as a generalized form of domination and control and able "to ignore anything that does not properly fit in with a logocentric system of knowledge" (Fiumara 1990: 6). It exercises a supreme legislative power that establishes proper ways of thinking. Western (intellectual) culture has a strong need to keep all interactive forms closely bound within a network of cognitive categories considered 'normal' and practicable.

---

[21]   However, this does not mean that the question should not be asked, as Gadamer makes clear. The only thing that should be acknowledged is that asking, besides openness, also implies limitation (Gadamer 1979: 330).

[22]   Poststructuralist ideas on ethics and spirituality seem to merge here: both emphasize an openness to the other and to otherness, the latter being a force (a 'minority' in Deleuzian terms) that traverses the logic and knowledge of logocentric thinking.

Fiumara's alternative hinges on the possibility of "freeing our thinking from its constitutive compulsion to submit to analyze, scrutinize, delve into, explore, exhaust, probe the famous 'object of knowledge' of our research tradition" (Fiumara 1990: 16). How? By giving back to Western thought the other half of language, namely, the rich openness of listening. Through listening we create a defense against any form of logocratic terrorism which may enslave the mind. Fiumara hastens to say that this does not mean that listening opposes the tradition of Western logos; it only refrains from excommunicating anything that 'normal' rationality is unable to grasp or systematize. Instead, it creates ever new spaces in the very place in which it is carried out (Fiumara 1990: 19).[23] Listening can be an important support to the effort of seeking to establish a relationship between our world and a different world, a polyphonic world where all the different voices, with their various resonances and intonations, can resound and reverberate. The listening approach Fiumara advocates may break up closed discourses and de- and reorganize the most rigidly constituted theoretical and institutional frames. It is almost as though in order to listen one must become different, since it is not so much a grasping of concepts or propositions as it is attempting an experience.[24] Unless we are ready, receptive, and also, possibly, vulnerable, the experience of listening appears to be impossible (Fiumara 1990: 191).[25]

---

[23] Already in the chapters on John Coltrane and Arvo Pärt, I observed that real listening is only possible when someone adopts a humble and passible attitude. Following Heidegger, man should not try to be the master of Being but its guardian or keeper, obedient, awaiting, and open to what announces itself. For Heidegger, to think first of all means to listen, to be able to listen.

[24] According to Alan Watts, listening relates in any way badly to thinking: "To understand music, you must listen to it. But so long as you are thinking, 'I am listening to this music,' you are not listening" (Watts 1951: 87). Rethinking Descartes' famous statement 'Cogito, ergo sum,' Peter Sloterdijk comes to the conclusion that this thinking subject is in fact founded in the ability to hear himself, that is, to hear the inner sound of thinking itself. It is a *sonorous Cogito*, an 'I-hear-it-speak-in-me' that precedes the Cogito. However, this only comes to light when the subject does not intend anything with his thoughts. To explain, to prove, to achieve – all this interferes with the aural relation to the topical thoughts traversing the subject. He already 'thinks' of something different than the whispering sound of present thinking. He who hears the sounding within himself, cannot construct at the same time (Sloterdijk 1993: 338).

[25] Fiumara attaches great importance to the idea of *Gelassenheit*, of letting-be. Reformulating this Heideggerian concept, *Gelassenheit* for Fiumara implies an attitude which occupies no space but which continually creates new spaces. In the moment in which we 'arm' ourselves with cognitive models we are, paradoxically, justified in losing interest in the object. We no longer consider it as enigmatic since it is our turn to speak to it; the object no longer has very much to say to us (Fiumara 1990: 19 and 106). *Gelassenheit* as a listening attitude is a way out of indifference; instead it is depicted as an attitude in the face of which nothing is simple or natural.

Whereas Heidegger first of all seems to be promoting a pre-conceptual listening, Fiumara advocates a listening attitude beyond concepts, outside identification, objectification, and recognition. In my opinion, it is exactly in this disoriented stance that listening achieves a spiritual dimension; that it becomes an opening for the spiritual, for the specific contingencies, complexities, and mysteries of our existence as material beings in a material world; that it introduces us to the incommensurability of being and thought, of category and reality, of language and being.[26] Mark you, this aural attentiveness and susceptibility is not radically opposed to other listening attitudes, to structural listening for example: it announces itself *through* these other modes. It traverses as an uninvited guest, that is, beyond all intentionalities, the listening skills required to sustain logocentrism. It disrupts the existing systems of regulation and order and confronts us with their inevitable inadequacies.[27] The results of certain activities of composers and musicians can sometimes instigate such a listening attitude. We turn our heads, furrow our brows, burst into laughter; we get goose bumps, become confused and dislocated, have to move or stand rooted to the spot. *It* happens, but only if we are open and receptive, that is, in a state between activity and passivity. The thus suggested rethinking of spirituality does not lead to an aesthetization of the spiritual; rather, our being in relation with art (music) exceeds the mere aesthetical and touches a trace of something that can no longer be understood in or through an aesthetical terminology. This 'something' – which can, as I argue throughout this book, be called the spiritual – becomes experienceable through music, through our encounter with music, through listening to and fro music.

Is sound privileged here? In other words, in (listening to) music, is one in a better position to experience the spiritual than, for example, in regarding the visual?

---

[26]   Within this context, it might even be possible to connect Adorno's plea for respectful listening with his critique of the social structure, sometimes described as a method of 'listening for dissonance.' For Adorno, the task of the social critic is to listen for sounds of disharmony, to catch the moments of discord and discrepancy and to make audible the contradictions, the untruths, toward which the dissonance is calling our attention (Levin 1989: 101–2). Maybe Adorno's listening to dissonances should not only be read and understood as a social or political criticism but, on another level, as a listening to what sounds (music) might have to say to us outside or beyond the current and accepted ways of approaching and experiencing music. The listening attitude Adorno advocates can thus be connected to some kind of resistance by shifting the focus to breakdowns, ruptures, and 'the unsayable' in our current modes and institutions of communication, of communicating about music. We could thus interpret his idea on 'real listening' as a deconstruction of any (other) non-critical listening. Or, to formulate it more cautiously, his predilection for a certain type of attentive listening could inherently constitute some resistance to the reification of communicatively structured domains of action, and perhaps this resistance would generate some possibilities for changing the communicative infrastructures within which we live.
[27]   Listening respects "the erotic power of ambiguity," writes Paul Carter (Erlmann 2004: 61).

Is the ear indeed the most spiritually determined of the senses as Søren Kierkegaard states in *Enten-Eller* [*Either/Or*]? Although visual experiences, just like aural ones, can permeate the whole body (the skin 'sees,' the eyes 'feel'), there does seem to be an important difference. In *Nada Brahma*, Joachim-Ernst Berendt distinguishes the field of the gaze (as being exterior) from the range of hearing (as being depth). The eye explores surfaces, whereas the ear cannot discern anything that does not penetrate. The eye analyzes, divides, rules, and is directed towards the mind; the ear, on the contrary, is receptive and intuitive; it belongs to the spirit and perceives the whole as one (Berendt 1990: xix–xx).[28] Though less esoteric, Peter Sloterdijk assumes a similar distinction. In his essay 'Wo sind wir, wenn wir Musik hören?' ['Where Are We, When We Listen to Music'] he ascertains a spatial chasm between the subject who sees and the object that is seen, a chasm that is also ontological. The ocular subjectivity implies a not-involved witnessing, a necessary distance, an external relationship: the seeing subject can be located at the edge of the world. Conversely, the ear has no opposite; it does not develop a frontal 'sighting' of an object located at some, however small, distance (Sloterdijk 1993: 319).[29] Heidegger's ideas on *inter-esse*, to be among things, resonate in Sloterdijk's analysis: listening means being-in-sound, being amidst the acoustic event.[30] It is this ontological involvement, subsistent in aural experiences, which can initiate a contact beyond the control of the eye, a contact at a threshold where one sheds the mastery of the I/eye (see Threshold 1), a contact with the inexhaustible richness of that which surrounds us. We are first of all summoned to listen to the call of the spiritual, the call of a material, everyday spirituality. According to Sloterdijk, music that corresponds to this listening attitude can be called *exodus music* (whereas *sedative music* makes every effort not to hear the world and otherness).

Where are we when we listen to music? The location remains vague; it is only certain that, while listening to music, one can never be completely in-the-world. To listen to music means either to move towards the world or to flee from it, either to be on the way there or on the way back. In both cases, however, listening suggests wandering, erring, groping. For me, the latter option can be connected to a spiritual quest, longing for security, safety, and wholeness. The former refers to an other spirituality, one that accepts insecurity, otherness, and heterogeneity. It is this idea of spirituality that I wished to track down in this book – through music, because it was precisely music that put me on that track.

---

[28] According to Berendt, the symbol of the ear is the shell, which also symbolizes the female genitals, themselves a symbol of reception and acceptance.

[29] "Vision is a spectator; hearing is a participation," John Dewey already wrote in 1927 in *The Public and Its Problems*.

[30] Sloterdijk correctly emphasizes that he is describing here a more or less ideal situation. In reality, most people relate to the audible in the same way as to visible, distant objects: absentminded, unaffected, objectifying, in a mode of self-protection and distancing (Sloterdijk 1993: 320).

THRESHOLD 12
Para-spirituality

WHERE has this wandering, this groping and erring taken us? Which (new) perspectives have been opened by the de- and reterritorialization of spirituality through many different musics? Which (new) listening attitudes towards many different musics have been opened through a reconsideration of the concept of spirituality? What has the rethinking of the relationship between music and spirituality brought in?

Perhaps crossing all these thresholds and plodding along deserts, islands and other far-off corners has lead to another beginning, another point of departure indicating that music can, at most, provide the opportunity for an experience which might be adorned with the adjective spiritual instead of being spiritual itself. In other words, spirituality is not an intrinsic characteristic of (certain) music;[1] it withdraws from the power of a musical work, from human capacities. Instead, spirituality refers to a relating, a certain relation between a subject (a listener, a musician) and an object (music), a relation which is at the same time possible and impossible, necessary and contingent, enforced and unverifiable.[2] This does

---

[1] In this sense, Monsignor Marco Frisina's advanced plans to compose the soundtrack for a stage version of Dante's *Divine Comedy* is a missed opportunity. Frisina plans to use blistering punk, metal, and jazz to signify hell, while gentle classical aria's after the fashion of Donizetti and Bellini illustrate paradise and mystical Gregorian chants mark Purgatory, thereby confirming most (contemporary) prejudices concerning the alleged spiritual characteristics of very specific music: only certain music can be holy, religious, or spiritual.

Frisina's sketches sharply contrast the *Notes sur la peinture d'aujourd'hui* from 1948 by the French painter Jean Bazaine. In this work, Bazaine asserts that specific religious art does not exist. Art can only contribute authentically to the existence of a community when it expresses the spiritual or the sacred in an autonomous way, that is, in or through its own medium. Bazaine's line of thinking somehow echoes the influential treatise *Über das Geistige in der Kunst* [*Concerning the Spiritual in Art*] of Russian-French artist Wassily Kandinsky. In this work from 1912, Kandinsky mentions a spiritual dimension of art that can be achieved through purely artistic means alone. According to Kandinsky, the elementary physical impressions of art are of importance simply as gestures towards the spiritual. A picture is therefore well painted only if its spiritual value is complete and satisfying. In that sense, it is essential for the artist to correctly gauge his position, to realize that he has a duty to his art and to himself, and that he is 'only' a servant of a nobler purpose. In his essay Kandinsky makes clear that, for him, literature, music and art are the primary and most sensitive spheres in which the spiritual makes itself felt.

Kandinsky's and Bazaine's thoughts seem to skim along the equation of spiritual qualities with particular intrinsic characteristics of certain art works, a basic assumption I have disputed throughout this book. Nevertheless, I sympathize with their ideas that art is able to give a specific entrance to traces of the spiritual, thereby not only detaching it from religion but also rethinking its appearances.

[2] If attentive listening is a crucial condition for a musical spirituality to become experienceable (see Threshold 11), certain modes of interacting among musicians might perhaps be considered as traces of the spiritual as well. I am thinking here about musical, interactive and (thus) social connections based on risk, vulnerability, and trust during the course of performances that exceed the conscious technical input of the individual musicians separately, a communication process that necessarily involves a careful listening

not imply the conscious choice of a subject, at least not only. That would bring us back to Adorno's ideas on a subject who rules, to his confidence in the constituting syntheses of a listening individual. Spiritual experiences take place at the limits of human consciousness. In effect, they never take place as such. They do not take place within consciousness; they exceed human consciousness, and that is why they can be terrifying (V. Taylor 1999: 97). Although these experiences require a certain activity on the subject's part, they cannot be confined to the active will of a subject (be it a composer or a listener). Rather, to experience the relation between music and spirituality calls for both a passive and an active attitude. It means to be receptive to the advent of an otherness, to receive and to be received by that otherness, to allow the coming of a still unanticipatable alterity for which no horizon of waiting as yet seems ready, in place, available. Yet it is necessary to prepare for it; for in order to allow the coming of the spiritual, passivity, a certain kind of resigned passivity by which everything is experienced as sameness, is not suitable. Letting the other come is not inertia open to anything whatsoever. One must make ready for the spiritual, create a space to let it come, come in (Derrida 1989: 55–6).[3] This way of listening – passive in its dedication to the music that presents itself and active in its alertness to and preparedness for an alterity – constantly jeopardizes the self-consciousness of a subject, the domination of an identity secured by the exclusion of difference.[4] The other concept of spirituality that has emerged – a concept that has revealed itself through several encounters with music – refers to an openness, a receptivity for that which withdraws from

---

to non-verbal and non-syntactical sounds produced by fellow musicians. Musicians often describe such moments as 'ESP' (extrasensory perception), something that 'just happens' or 'taking the music to another level.' ('Groove' might also be a good example here of how this experience is named.)

What I would like to make clear with this supplementary comment is that spirituality always transcends the self. In that sense, we should also take into consideration the notion that spirituality is not about the interior but about the exterior, about departure and, therefore, about a fundamental instability of personal identity. Spirituality occurs or happens in and through connections to the world, to other people, to music.

Instead of thinking that the spiritual must be dug up and discovered somewhere deep inside of us, music points us in another direction, outward – spirituality as that which transcends our individuality and joins us with the world at large (Solomon 2002: 134).

   3   Derrida's reflections on this kind of hospitality, this kind of ethics, are very close to what Heidegger sets apart with the verb 'to perceive.' For Heidegger, to perceive means the same thing as to receive and is pointing toward perception in the sense of receptivity, as distinguished from the spontaneity with which we assume this or that attitude toward what we perceive. "To perceive implies […] to welcome and to take in; to accept and take in the encounter" (Heidegger 1968: 61). In the same way he considers proper hearing as the ability to pay thoughtful attention to simple things.

   4   In my opinion, the subject is an energetic junction through which information constantly flows, a subject having reason at its disposal as one of the possibilities to channel communication. Not only are subjects formed only in interaction with others, they ultimately *are* that interaction, that network of relations.

reassuring strategies of domination and nomination. However, it needs a particular disposition, a vital and creative power (spirit), to become experienceable; it needs a breath of life (spirit), inspiration, a tuning and detuning simultaneously. Otherwise it remains imperceptible to the human mind and senses (spirit).

Referring to an alterity, to experiences exceeding the domination of a sovereign subject, does not mean that the concept of spirituality as presented throughout this book is other-worldly. To experience the spiritual does not require a firm belief in transcendental powers, nor can it be restricted to religious values. However, it is not understandable through Western logocentrism either, with its presupposed unambiguity and clearly delimiting, hierarchically organized, binary opposites.

If spirituality escapes any presentation within logocentrism, if it only leaves traces, and if sensing that it can always only leave traces is in itself a certain kind of spiritual experience, then it can not be recuperated through logocentric thinking. One might say that it is transcendent to this way of thinking, transcendent to presentation. At the same time, however, this transcendence no longer refers to an 'other world'; it is situated within the immanent. So, here, the word transcendence does not stand for the result of a movement beginning with sensory perceptions and arriving somewhere above or beyond the sensual; rather, the transcendent should be considered a present participle, referring to the idea that, from the beginning, there is a tension, a fissure, or a deficiency between our experiences and their representations. This leads to the conviction that, in a certain way, questions concerning spirituality and music must remain unanswered, at any rate without a general and rule-governed response, without a response other than that which is linked specifically each time to the occurrence of a decision without rules and without will in the course of a new test of the undecidable (Derrida 1992: 14).

The idea that spirituality is immanent, singular, and not otherworldly, encompasses another consequence. The concept of the spiritual as presented here does not indicate an already existing (ethereal) presence, elusive and incomprehensible, but nevertheless formed and ready to be discovered, approximated, or touched by (certain) music.[5] Although prevailing thoughts and intuitions concerning the spiritual might traverse certain experiences while

---

[5]   By inserting the adjective 'certain' here, it might still be suggested in the end that some specific music is more suitable for spiritual experiences than others. I don't disagree with this implication. However, this should not mean that we can decide in advance, in general, and for once and for all which music is more likely to give access to an alterity that could be called spiritual. In a way, this is of subjective concern or, better, a singular matter. It is of course the subject who chooses to listen to the music s/he likes. However, it is not a conscious exercise of one's will to arrive at spiritual experiences during the act of listening. Although the subject has to be active in a way to get ready for the spiritual (see above), *it happens* beyond her/his control. Furthermore, it is not at all sure that *it* will happen again and again with the same music. The subject is not a static being and the way s/he welcomes music is liable to changes. Also the context in which the music appears might differ considerably, which may alter the subject's perception of it.

encountering music, music only brings the spiritual into existence. A musical work can offer it the opportunity to appear. But spirituality does not precede the music; it is through music (and of course through many other evocations) that we encounter the spiritual, a different spirituality, each time different. A spiritual experience is therefore always mediated and thus never immediate. Spirituality is thus no stable concept, an invariable (and with that a definable) idea; spirituality *happens*, it happens each time differently and is therefore in a constant process of becoming, of (trans)formation. Spirituality is a movement.

By rethinking spirituality through certain musics, other encounters with those musics become possible, encounters that might be called spiritual. Music's power to reconsider spirituality makes it simultaneously possible to approach that same music in a different way. This way, however, can never be defined for once and for all; it is singular and immanent. The most we can say of it is that this way is twisting and not very well specified; more like traces in a desert, a smooth space, to be discovered time and again.

Following Victor Taylor, I would suggest calling the concept of spirituality presented in the previous chapters, a concept I could only arrive at through music, a *para-spirituality*. According to Deleuze and Guattari, Kafka has introduced a minor language – Taylor calls it a *para-grammar* – into the major language, a grammar which moves differently from the conventional language of his time, escaping its rules and supplanting the dominant structure of that major language by calling attention to its margins, its lapses, its contradictions and by bearing witness to the unlocalized presence of an indirect discourse at the heart of every assertion. Para-grammar makes a major language stammer by negotiating all its variables (V. Taylor 1999: 14; Deleuze and Guattari 1987: 104–5). In much the same way, I deem para-spirituality as an outside always already on the inside, an inflection of the spiritual as we usually regard it, a postmodern version of the Kantian *par-ergon*.[6]

So, although not all music may be capable of evoking spiritual experiences at all times, one cannot exclude from any music the possibility that it arouses at a certain moment a susceptibility in the subject which I would call spiritual. However, this should not be read as a plea for artistic accessibility, that is, a conforming to certain (compositional) conventions, thereby creating a self-assured audience. Music lovers aren't required to abdicate their certitudes completely. But certitude and artistic discipline reach their limits, the limits of the undisciplined and the uncertain, there where a spiritual experience becomes possible. The music I am talking about is not accessible 'just like that'; it attracts, it fascinates, and, simultaneously, it withdraws and refuses access.

6   "A parergon comes against, beside, and in addition to the *ergon*, the work done, the fact, the work, but it does not fall to one side, it touches and cooperates within the operation, from a certain outside. Neither simply outside nor simply inside" (Derrida 1978: 54). In other words, the parergon undermines opposites, inside vs. outside, intrinsic vs. extrinsic, essential vs. accidental, and so on.

'Para' is the dangerous prefix defying the rules of identity, stability, and centricity while finding difference in sameness or sameness in difference, signifying at once proximity and distance, similarity and disparity, interiority and exteriority. It indicates a subsidiary state of being or the indeterminacy of a word or action. 'Para' is concerned with a word or action before it finds its rule, its inside and outside, its frame. It suspends the instantiation of the word itself (para-spirituality defers spirituality): as such it belongs to the logic of *paralogy* – beside, aside from, or beyond reason. It is an intervention within the prescriptive rules, categories, and grammar of the dominant discourse. Like the 'post' in post-modernism, it precedes the word to designate the after, and at the same time it brings forth the darker and more threatening anteriorities of the word. 'Para' defers the meaning of the word in order to prevent the action from taking language (V. Taylor 1999: 17).

Since metaphysics (understood as the intellectual vision of ideas anchored to the stability of reality's essential structures) has unmasked itself as an untenable and inefficacious belief because of an inexorable proliferation of world 'pictures,' the fragmentation of life spheres, and the *de facto* order of the rationalized world of modern technological societies (Vattimo 2002: 14–15), a postmodern conceptualization and experientialization of para-spirituality, destabilizing any notion of ultimacy, everlasting Truth and supreme Being, is needed to replace a metaphysically grounded spirituality. Para-spirituality appears after 'the death of God,' interpreted by Gianni Vattimo as the absence of an ultimate foundation or ground as well as the loss of credence in an objective truth, orienting rather toward a perspective that conceives of truth as an effect of power (Vattimo 2002: 3 and 105).[7]

Immanuel Kant uses the word parergon in his text *Die Religion innerhalb der Grenzen der bloßen Vernunft* [*Religion within the Limits of Reason Alone*] to describe certain parts of religion that are not integral parts of religion, but rather verge on it. In fact, Kant describes here the limits of thought and Reason. Reason 'knows' as it were that there is more to say about religion than it can grasp or appropriate. Kant mentions in particular the effects and means of grace, miracles, and mysteries (in short, the unfathomable field of the supernatural), but also adds corresponding detriments to these four types of religious parerga: fanaticism, thaumaturgy, superstition, and illuminism. However, he admits, these four aberrations or seductions of reason also contain and bring forth a certain pleasing, pleasing-God (Derrida 1978: 55–6).

[7]   According to Vattimo, Nietzsche's declaration of God's decease is therefore

… not an atheistic thesis like 'God does not exist.' Nietzsche could not state a thesis like the nonexistence of God because the claim to its absolute truth would have to be upheld as a metaphysical principle, that is, as the true 'structure' of reality, having the same function as the traditional God of metaphysics. (Vattimo 2002: 3)

In much the same way Vattimo criticizes the Levinasian and Derridean idea of God as the wholly other. This God, too, who in absolute transcendence overwhelms thought, can only be conceived of in metaphysical terms. But, Vattimo states, one cannot remove a foundation

Rationalization, technology, and a scientific world view have dismantled a belief in a metaphysical God, regarded as the ultimate *telos* of the world, as useless and obsolete. The pluralistic world in which we live cannot be interpreted by an ideology that seeks to unify it at all costs in the name of one sole Truth.

Like Georges Bataille, Vattimo tries to salvage a certain belief which I would like to call para-spiritual. Bataille's para-spirituality is engrafted onto the attempt to redeem the spiritual from reason. With 'the death of God,' man does not enter a humanist universe, but an empty space, in which he can rely neither upon God nor upon himself. We should come to realize that we are not able to appropriate what passes over us. In *Le coupable* Bataille writes that man becomes divine precisely in the experience of his limits. God is not man's limit, but man's limits are divine (Bataille 1973: 350). Spirituality becomes enclosed in the idea that certain experiences take man to his limits, of which God is no longer the incarnation. Bataille's reflections on God's absence (negative) immediately transform into reflections on God-as-absentee (positive). He proclaims an openness for the dizziness of a world without God, for the whimsical vicissitudes of our existence, for the disorganized flux of being. Man thus enters a spiritual fringe.

Likewise, Vattimo's *para-catholic* spirituality does not possess the stability assigned to the spirituality of metaphysical tradition. Rather, it gives itself again and again, in its occurrences. With this, Vattimo places himself within the tradition of hermeneutical theology: religion and spirituality are in a constant process of becoming, of transformation. His para-spirituality is a liberating leap into the abyss; liberating because of destabilizing the claim that the order of beings should be held as the eternal and objective order of Being, a claim which Vattimo calls the violence of metaphysics. It is exactly the dissolution of metaphysics that generates an openness to (renewed) spiritual experiences (Vattimo 2002: 26). In other words, a spirituality that presents itself anew in our culture must abandon the project of grounding its ethics upon an assumed knowledge of natural essences established as norms. Approvingly, Vattimo cites Heidegger who states that what is decisive is not spiritual contemplation, its specific strains, and its concrete promise of redemption, but the endurance of weakness throughout one's life. This weakness reveals itself in an infinite procreation of interpretation, a strolling and erring that never reaches a final destination or unquestionable truth.

Thinking further along these lines, para-spirituality might refer to the absence of a singular predominating value of the spiritual, of ultimacy; expressions of ultimacy can only exist as a space-between or as a limit-concept drawing attention to the inherent lack of completeness present in human apprehension: Bataille's empty space or Foucault's *atopos* (see Threshold 5). Para-spirituality is thus an erring or a wandering around the 'not' or 'not there,' though not comparable to a negative theology because it lacks a presupposition of any transcendental signified:

in the name of anti-foundationism only to reinstate a foundation that is more pleasing to an array of ideological formations.

"The question of the not is the question of the unthinkable that we can neither think nor not think. In thinking not, thought approaches a limit that inhabits it as if from within. This exteriority, which is interior, rends thought, leaving it forever incomplete" (M. Taylor 1993: 1). However, the 'not here' is not necessarily a 'there' and the 'not there' is not necessarily a 'here.' The 'not (t)here' does not function dialectically or reciprocally; it is an inaccessible space, the space of the *para*, arising in between the 'here' and 'there.'[8]

Para-spirituality takes place but has no place, no place proper to it. It has no proper time too, that is, no time proper to it apart from the local, particular, and immanent; the temporality and spatiality of spirituality is constantly shifting. This means that an experience of the para-spiritual can only exceed (and must exceed) the order of theoretical determination, of knowledge, of certainty; it is a productive void where no fixed thoughts remain (Derrida 1993: 20).

In my opinion, it is music that plays an important role in the debate encompassing the end of metaphysics, providing the basis for a critical evaluation of the traces by which (the rebirth of) spirituality appears in our time.

Music questions and deconstructs (Western) logocentric oppositions throughout history. Arvo Pärt's *Sarah Was Ninety Years Old* orbits around that empty place called silence. 'Hotel California' sings of the abandoning of control. Identity and self-consciousness are undermined through the effects of the Sirens' songs. Schumann and Dave Douglas are aural wanderers, revealing the undecidability present in various musical structures. Through his abysmal music, John Coltrane searches the unattainable. These were the acoustical landmarks along which a thinking developed, opening a space for the para-spiritual. These were the anchorages where music became (linked to the) para-spiritual. These were a few stopping places on the path of rethinking spirituality through music.

So, if para-spirituality, as stated above, is about groping, hesitating, searching, not-knowing, about abutting onto, brushing against, and intervening within, about the insight that the spiritual is unable to contain itself within itself and therefore needs the para-spiritual, about the spiritual in the absence of an absolute exteriority, it should pay attention not (only) to God but to the Devil (as well), not to Gabriel but to Lucifer, not to Peter but to Judas, not to Mother Mary but to Mary Magdalene, not to the Immaculate Conception but to promiscuity.

---

[8] In Threshold 2, I referred to Maurice Blanchot and Friedrich Hölderlin, both writing of a space between the divine and the human world. The late Hölderlin realizes that the attempts of the poet to serve as an intermediary between man and God have become impossible. And the artwork (poem) is no longer the place where the divine can emerge. Instead, the poet should allow for a separation between the spheres of the divine and the human – no communion but an autonomy of difference. That empty space between the two spheres, not here and not there – that space *is* the spiritual; spirituality is the intimacy of the gap.

"I don't know how to love him."[9] Although Mary Magdalene sighs she is a woman with enough experience ("I've had so many men before, in very many ways"[10]), she does not know what to do with Jesus. This time it is different. Old, well-known tricks no longer work: Jesus acts atypically. Moreover, she is no longer satisfied with the role she has been playing: her body at everybody's disposal, her mind switched off. And flowing from this, she does not recognize herself anymore: she used to be the one in control of the situation, but now the situation seems to be controlling her (see Ex. 12.1).

Mary's double despair, however, contrasts sharply with the simple melody and harmonic structure. 'I don't know how to love him' is the most tender song of *Jesus Christ Superstar*. She cannot express her worries in the same way Jesus, Judas and the other disciples can: she cannot disturb Jesus once he is finally sleeping, totally exhausted from the people pulling at him from all sides (a pragmatic and altruistic argument). She cannot openly aim for a privileged position near Jesus on the basis of love; she cannot aim for it because she is a woman, a woman, moreover, of questionable character (a socio-political argument). She cannot speak up, because she does not know what to say and how to say it: her encounter with Jesus has left her almost speechless (a psychological argument). In other words, melody, harmony, rhythm, and orchestration together perform the event of Mary's (inner) voice being silenced. The sole and brief outburst ("Should I bring him down, should I scream and shout ..."[11]) is enveloped and immediately disarmed by a sugary melody accompanied by an acoustic guitar.

The figure of Mary Magdalene in *Jesus Christ Superstar* seems to provide a representation, as a sort of classical fusion, of many women, many Maries, acting in the Bible. First, she is portrayed as a follower of Jesus, a true disciple who, nevertheless, does not belong to the group of Apostles immediately surrounding Jesus. She acts more as a hanger-on and a servant, both to Jesus and the Twelve. In this sense, she can be called a *para-disciple*, both outside as well as part of the inner circle of confidants. Second, when she tells Jesus in 'Everything's Alright' that she will minister unto him and treat him with expensive ointments, she becomes identified with the repentant sinner at the house of Simon the Pharisee (Luke 7:36–50). Tim Rice, accountable for the lyrics, and Norman Jewison, the movie director, follow here Pope Gregory the Great's pronouncement from 591 AD in which Mary Magdalene and Luke's unchaste woman are identified as one and the same person (an idea not confirmed by authentic sources and contemporary exegesis). Third, the possession of perfumes and her loose hair (with which she will dry Jesus' feet) are signs of a fallen woman. With these paraphernalia in combination with the text "And I've had so many men before, in very many ways. He's just one more,"[12] the opera contributes to the aura of sexuality which envelops Mary Magdalene.

9   Lyrics © 1970 by MCA Music Ltd, London.
10   Ibid.
11   Ibid.
12   Ibid.

Example 12.1 'I don't know how to love him', mm 1–10 © MCA Music Ltd.

Belief and love, spiritual contemplation and physical attraction, mental and corporal dedication merge or conflict, leaving her forever on a threshold. Fourth, Jesus' reply to Judas' criticism of Mary in 'Strange Thing Mystifying' weaves in yet another story, the Woman Taken in Adultery (John 8:1–11). When Judas brings up Mary's dubious profession and sexually tinted behavior, Jesus replies irritated: "If your slate is clean, then you can throw stones. If your slate is not, then leave her alone,"[13] a modern version of his response to the scribes and Pharisees who wanted to stone the sinner without a name. Throughout this famous 1971 rock opera, Mary is repeatedly compared with and referred to as a prostitute, a sinful woman whose repentance and conversion cannot convince everybody. Living in a space between whore, servant and saint, she can never be more than a para-saint.

Just as in the *Wirkungsgeschichte*, the effective history of the gospels, a conflation of several women into a single figure takes place in *Jesus Christ Superstar*.[14] The tension and ambiguity between coquetry and penance present in the figure of Mary Magdalene, so easily traceable within the histories of Christianity, also permeate this opera. Mary Magdalene confronts us with a space between the religious and the profane: neither religious nor profane and, simultaneously, religious and profane – undecidable, unthinkable within the major language of Christianity.

However, history shows a growing attention to, elevation in importance of, and rising devotion to Mary Magdalene which, in my opinion, contributes to the workings of the para-spiritual, understood here as an approximated ultimacy, or, better, an

---

[13] Lyrics © 1970 by MCA Music Ltd, London.

[14] It is not my intention to unravel and rectify this conflation. Rather, I am interested in examining the influence and effects of texts, be they academic or literary, high-brow or popular, historical or fictional; as such, I wish to take seriously the depiction of biblical figures in films and music.

ultimacy of approximation.[15] Re-interpreting her appearance, she is no counterpoint to an absolute good, no necessary negativity against which true goodness can be revealed, no moment of de-sacralization but a moment of the para-sacred.

In *Jesus Christ Superstar*, the para-spiritual emerges as the becoming-woman. Alongside the criticism mentioned above (Mary is silenced in the process of emoting her true feelings), another reading of Mary Magdalene's position is possible. She is the only female in the opera whose voice sounds, and her role is far more prominent than those of the main disciples Peter, James, and John. She declares herself to Jesus, she takes care of him while he is disputing with Judas thereby underplaying logos ("She alone has tried to give me, what I need right here and now,"[16] Jesus says), and she reproves Peter after his denial ("Peter, don't you know what you have said, you've done and cut him dead"[17]). The opera centers around Jesus, Judas, and Mary Magdalene, thereby providing a significant space for the para-spiritual and the feminine, for the para-spiritual *as* the feminine. Granted, Mary is represented as a prostitute and para-disciple, but she is not condemned. On the contrary: more than once throughout the opera, Jesus is shown to protect her. And in her rebuking of Peter, she appears not as villainous bitch but rather as the Apostola Apostolorum.

Could this be interpreted as a certain reinstatement of the feminine? Women, so important at the origins of the Apostolic community, were gradually displaced and depreciated, especially in the circles from which the Imperial, orthodox Church developed. Although the gospels clearly show that Christ regards his women followers as disciples in their own right, capable of receiving unique revelation and worthy of being valid witnesses to his death, burial, and resurrection, by the end of the second century the egalitarian principles defined in the New Testament have been discarded in favor of a return to the patriarchal system of Judaism which preceded it. And by the third century, the Church has settled scores with the richness and diversity of beliefs co-existing in early Christianity and has imposed a common system of teaching and ritual on the scattered Christian communities, binding them together in the 'one Catholic and apostolic church' (Haskins 1993: 30–56). In other words, the more the ordering structures prevail, the more men come to the fore. They crowd out women and, simultaneously, the (para-)spiritual capacities of most ordinary humans. However, given the important role women play in the gospel events and, more specifically, in the spiritual journey undertaken by Jesus – helping to bring about transformations in his personality, enriching his

---

[15]   Just as Kant needs extensive footnotes to describe four moments that belong to religion yet are no integral part of it (see footnote 6), spirituality needs the para-spiritual to the extent that the inside is lacking. It needs the supplement. And this additive is threatening: biblical figures seem to point back to their origin and destination, much like signs with a transcendent referent. However, in moments of para-spirituality, the figures often also point in other directions. The pointing back is incomplete and subject to deviation (V. Taylor 1999: 101).

[16]   Lyrics © 1970 by MCA Music Ltd, London.

[17]   Ibid.

perceptions and behavior – a reorientation and reevaluation of their position is necessary. This rethinking, however, should not be so much of an emancipation, an equal treatment of two opposing forces; rather, what should become clear is that in the heart of a primarily male Christianity, the female is always already present, always already active, as a force that offers resistance to the major language.

The para-spiritual (defined by variation, heterogeneity, creativity) is not opposed to the spiritual (defined by constants, homogeneity, systems). The former is engrafted in the latter, always already a part of it, yet separable from it: the extra-being or being between. The 'para' refers to a strange proliferation of shifting effects, a taste for overload and paraphrase, a dissolution of constant form in favor of differences. It cannot be governed by a code, a law, or a rule, and functions, incalculable and unpredictable, on the margins of everything that can be determined as Being, One, Whole, or God. The power of the para-spiritual does not lie in its capability to become spiritual, but in its subverting influences on all kinds of existing models. The para-spiritual is a threshold, a bridge. The presentation of Mary Magdalene in *Jesus Christ Superstar*, moving between faith and love, confidence and hesitation, independence and loyalty, materiality and immateriality, sexuality and spirituality, testifies to this trope.

THRESHOLD 13
The Bridge and the Laugh

Engaging music has led me to rethink the (para-)spiritual as a moving between known and knowable forms. Neither becoming transparent through rational thinking nor remaining connected to a belief in metaphysical powers, spirituality, I proposed, might be considered an experience of an *inter-esse*, literally a being-between, something that happens in a space between, untimely and atopical.[1] As such, it surpasses fixed (oppositions of) identities. Like a threshold. Like an interval as well. The separate components forming the interval remain audible, but something new has, at the same time, installed itself between them; the interval enters our ears without being reduced directly to its separate elements.[2] Neither the one nor the other. Like a bridge, simply another manifestation of the in-between. A bridge is an intermediary member, a *Mittelglied*, belonging neither to this side nor to the other side and at the same time to both. It should be treated as a separable part, a particular part, but also as a nonparticular, nondetachable part. The bridge is a threshold. It joins by separating and separates by joining. Connecting this side with the other side, no conclusion can be made as to which side the bridge itself belongs. It belongs to the space between, between here and there, between this world and that other world, between the known and the unknown. The bridge is a place of transition, but with its own dynamics, its own intensity, its own volume.

'Die Brücke' ['The bridge'] is the title of one of the numbers created during a collaboration between Lebanese *oud* player Rabih Abou-Khalil and German jazz pianist Joachim Kühn. The 2005 project is an encounter between two musical worlds or musical languages – each highly hybrid itself – which continually averts the one absorbing or disappearing into the other: sounds of one side reach the other side only as transformed and jumbled like a receding echo. 'Die Brücke' is music of the in-between, a transversal music that sweeps one and the other away, "coming and going rather than starting and finishing" (Deleuze and Guattari 1987: 25). Undermining its banks, 'Die Brücke' makes a dialogue audible in which all participants (Abou-Khalil and Kühn are accompanied here by drummer Jarrod Cagwin) leave their safe and known positions in order to meet in a space as yet unexplored and undefined: both jazz and Arabic music and simultaneously neither jazz nor Arabic music. The composition consists mainly of an improvisation on F before the musicians change during the last minute to a coda played in unison which, as concerns the melodic and rhythmic material, is quite distinct from the foregoing. West, the piano, and East, the *oud*, exchange ideas, support and stimulate each other; they join and challenge each other's vocabulary in a permanent fragility of meaning, inventing the message at the same time as the

---

[1]   Instead of the term 'para-spirituality' I could also have introduced the terms 'material spirituality' or 'ecological spirituality'. All these terms should make clear that the relation of a subject to its environment can no longer be grounded on a divine or cosmic *nomos*.

[2]   "The experience of my reader shall be between the phrases, in the silence, communicated by the intervals, not the terms, of the statement," Samuel Beckett writes in *Disjecta*.

language: a realm of fantastic insecurity. Doing solely for the sake of doing, for their pleasure, the musicians frolic in a light breeze that scarcely disturbs the air.[3]

'Die Brücke' is a sonic bridge. Like drifters repeatedly deviating from the normal, ordinary, lawful course, way, or path, these musicians never arrive at an aural homeland. Free from every secure dwelling, they are unsettling and uncanny – parasites whose 'place' is always a para-site: liminal and marginal. Having forsaken the straight and narrow and given up all thought of return, they appear to be vagrants or renegades, subversives who break the (power of the) law. The act of transgression breaks, infringes, trespasses, and violates.

Entirely in accordance with the idiom surrounding the concept of spirituality, the first word of the album's title is 'journey,' implying 'traveling,' 'being in transit,' leaving the proper place of dwelling: from here to there, from the familiar to the unfamiliar. Abou-Khalil and Kühn's journey is not a safe trip, completely organized and visiting only renown places, but an expedition to undiscovered grounds; a journey, actually, with an unknown destination. (The spiritual journey is "a self-imposed exile from the solidity of things," De Certeau [1992: 105] writes.)

The intended goal, however, seems to crystallize in the second part of the title: a journey 'to the center.' Ah, so this will prove to be, after all, a quest for essence, an unchangeable and stable core. It may be a tough journey, but the reward will be high: a place in the center, knowable to itself, a powerful middle or top from which everything disseminates and is controlled, a place wherefrom contradictions are solved and oppositions dissolve. In Derridaen terms: a transcendental signified.

However, which center are Abou-Khalil and Kühn heading toward? The full title of their CD is *Journey to the Center of an Egg*. This absurd humoristic maneuver turns the whole search for a center into a perilous and ludicrous undertaking.[4] What is the center of an egg? Where is it? And how can we ever

---

[3]   A movement of the air, the blowing of the wind, breathing in, breathing out. Music is an art of sound, and sound is vibrating air. We experience music only because air vibrates. Air vibrates through the vocal cords or the cords of an instrument. Music goes with the wind. Not only the music of 'wind-instruments,' not only singing, but all music. French philosopher Luce Irigaray, the most important Western philosopher who incessantly points out the primacy of air (instead of Being), reminds us of the inner weavings of air and music: *Air*, "a piece of music, written for a single voice, accompanying words, melody ..." (Irigaray 1983: 12).

Breathing, breath, air, *pneuma* – the words are directly related to music as well as possible translations of spirit and *spiritus*. Pneumatology is the part of Christian theology dealing with the doctrine of the Holy Spirit. And according to Gianni Vattimo, spirituality is "something volatile, fleeting, of which thought lost the memory when it began conceiving of spirit as the evident and indubitable foundation of self-consciousness, up to Hegel's absolute spirit" (Vattimo 2002: 52). Spirituality and music are thus always already connected.

[4]   Judging by song titles like 'Little Camels' and 'No Plastic Cups, Please,' I am presupposing that *Journey to the Center of an Egg* has no direct religious motivations but is indeed meant to be ludicrous. I am presupposing that Abou-Khalil is not referring to

arrive there? Is the alleged spiritual spell, so often advanced in collaborations where 'East meets West' and so palpable in the first four words of the CD title, broken, dissipated by a burst of laughter? Are humor and laughing the antitheses of spirituality? Freud considers the laugh an expression that declines to harmonize with utility and that resists the methodical. In *Inner Experience*, Georges Bataille thinks of the laugh as a 'praxis' immediately connected to surrender, an expression revealing an insufficiency (of language, of mastery). Laughing withdraws itself from every systematic acting or knowing. The laugh is ecstatic and, as such, a lapsing in the direction of the unknown. In this sense it can be connected to one idea of (para-)spirituality that imbues this book: both the laugh and (para)spirituality testify of the gaps permeating knowledge and controllability.

According to Bataille, laughing is also a form, an extreme form, of commun(icat)ion: in the loss of 'the self' – ecstasy being the effect of the laugh – one comes face to face with 'the other,' one meets the other. However, the laugh does not lead to a merging; the laughers "are no more separate than are two waves, but their unity is as undefined, as precarious as that of the agitation of the waters" (Bataille 1988: 95–6). Laughing thus leads neither to a fusion (the one *in* the other) nor to communication regarded as an exchange between autonomous beings (the one *to* the other). Neither together nor alone. Through this kind of commun(icat)ion, through this heteronomy in which one relates to the other without incorporating the other, but also without keeping the other at a distance, the spiritual reveals itself, or, as Bataille calls it, a 'communauté sacrée,' functioning to bring man to his limits.

Journey to the Center of an Egg is music that bursts into laughter. Abou-Khalil and Kühn are laughing and thereby both committing themselves and jeopardizing each other's identity. In their inaudible reverberating laugh, a temporary, uncontrolled solidarity and a vulnerable, non-solid cohesion become apparent. Undergoing together and going down together – the laugh becomes just another manifestation of the in-between.

Journey to the Center of an Egg. In this roar, this chuckle, this hoot, a way towards an experience of the para-spiritual is opened. Music on a threshold … Musicians on a threshold … Listeners on a threshold …

---

some indigenous tribes for whom eggs are mythological symbols or function in religious rituals. An example of one such story arises from the Makiritare, a people living in southern Venezuela. Wanadi (God, the unknowable, the unseen force) has *Huehanna*, a huge and hollow egg with a heavy shell, hard as stone. *Huehanna* contains unborn people, brought down to Earth from Heaven by Wanadi. Wanadi wants to open *Huehanna* on the Earth, allowing its people to emerge and spread over the Earth. However, as the Earth is still possessed and ruled by Odosha, the master of evil, Wanadi and the good people in *Huehanna* must wait until Odosha dies (Civrieux 1980: 23–7).

So, let's laugh ... Let's laugh on a threshold, still on a threshold, the threshold of leaving a book ... (as if thresholds could even be crossed). Books (like this one) do not have an ending proper. Every sentence fights for a footnote; every full stop demands the status of a comma (Ugrešić 1996: 191). The only thing I could do here is leave fragile markers: conclusions are not warranted, perhaps a state of affairs, at the most. A work which has as its purpose to rethink spirituality through music cannot be a conclusive product consisting of finished, resolved, encompassed thinking; it sets up a way of thinking itself. Therefore, this writing remains unfinished, lingering in the transitory passage between origin and conclusion, vibrating between coming and going, at the articulation between what absents itself and what presents itself, so as to remain underway ... on a dark desert highway ... accompanied by music ... led by music ... called by music ...

"You can check out any time you like, but you can never leave ..."[5]

Bibliography

Abell, Arthur M., *Talks With Great Composers* (New York: Citadel Press, 1994).

Adorno, Theodor W., *Introduction to the Sociology of Music*, trans. E.B. Ashton (New York: Seabury Press, 1976).

Ake, David, *Jazz Cultures* (Berkeley, CA: University of California Press, 2002).

Attali, Jacques, *Noise: The Political Economy of Music*, trans. B. Massumi (Minneapolis, MN: University of Minnesota Press, 1985).

Badiou, Alain, *Ethics: An Essay on the Understanding of Evil*, trans. P. Hallward (New York: Verso, 2001).

Barthes, Roland, *Image Music Text* (London: Fontana Press, 1977).

Barthes, Roland, *Roland Barthes door Roland Barthes*, trans. M.J. van Nieuwstadt and H. Hoeks (Nijmegen: SUN, 1991).

Bataille, Georges, 'Le sacré au XXe siècle', in *Oeuvres complètes* VIII (Paris: Gallimard, 1970), pp. 187–9.

Bataille, Georges, *Le coupable*, in *Oeuvres complètes* IV (Paris: Gallimard, 1973).

Bataille, Georges, *Erotism: Death and Sensuality*, trans. M. Dalwood (San Francisco, CA: City Lights Books, 1986).

Bataille, Georges, *Inner Experience*, trans. L.A. Boldt (Albany, NY: SUNY Press, 1988).

Beckett, Samuel, *Ill Seen, Ill Said* (New York: Grove Press, 1995).

Benjamin, Walter, 'Agesilaus Santander' (1933), in *Zur Aktualität Walter Benjamin* (Frankfurt am Main: Suhrkamp, 1972), pp. 94–102.

Berendt, Joachim Ernst, *Nada Brahma. De wereld is geluid*, trans. L.W. Carp and H.C.J. van Heerikhuizen (Den Haag: East-West Publications, 1990).

Blanchot, Maurice, 'From Dread to Language', in *The Station Hill Blanchot Reader: Fiction and Literary Essays*, ed. George Quasha, trans. Lydia Davis, Paul Auster, Robert Lamberton (Barrytown, NY: Station Hill Press, 1999), pp. 343–59.

Bohlman, Philip V., *World Music: A Very Short Introduction* (Oxford: Oxford University Press, 2002).

Certeau, Michel de, *The Mystic Fable: The Sixteenth and Seventeenth Centuries*, trans. M.B. Smith (Chicago, IL: University of Chicago Press, 1992).

Civrieux, Marc de, *Watunna: An Orinoco Creation Cycle*, trans. D.M. Guss (San Francisco, CA: North Point Press, 1980).

Clarke, David, 'Parting Glances. Aesthetic Solace or Act of Complicity?', *The Musical Times* (1993), pp. 680–84.

Cook, Nicolas, 'Theorizing Musical Meaning', *Music Theory Spectrum*, 23/2 (2001), pp. 170–95.

Cumming, Naomi, *The Sonic Self: Musical Subjectivity and Signification* (Bloomington, IN: Indiana University Press, 2000).

De la Motte-Haber, Helga, *Musik und Religion* (Laaber: Laaber-Verlag, 2003).

Deleuze, Gilles and Guattari, Félix, *A Thousand Plateaus: Capitalism and Schizophrenia*, trans. B. Massumi (Minneapolis. MN: University of Minnesota Press, 1987).

Derrida, Jacques, *Of Grammatology*, trans. G.C. Spivak (Baltimore, MD: Johns Hopkins University Press, 1976).

Derrida, Jacques, *Writing and Difference*, trans. A. Bass (London/New York: Routledge, 1978).

Derrida, Jacques, *Dissemination*, trans. B. Johnson (Chicago, IL: University of Chicago Press, 1981a).

Derrida, Jacques, *Positions*, trans. A. Bass (Chicago, IL: University of Chicago Press, 1981b).

Derrida, Jacques, *The Truth in Painting*, trans. G. Bennington (Chicago, IL: University of Chicago Press, 1987).

Derrida, Jacques, *Limited Inc.* (Evanston, IL: Northwestern University Press, 1988).

Derrida, Jacques, 'Psyche: Inventions of the Other', in Lindsay Waters and Wlad Godzich (eds), *Reading De Man Reading* (Minneapolis, MN: University of Minnesota Press, 1989).

Derrida, Jacques, 'Passions: An Oblique Offering', in David Wood (ed.), *Derrida: A Critical Reader* (Oxford: Blackwell, 1992).

Derrida, Jacques, *Aporias: Dying, Awaiting (One Another) at the 'Limits of Truth'*, trans. Th. Dutoit (Stanford, CA: Stanford University Press, 1993).

Derrida, Jacques, *Acts of Religion* (London/New York: Routledge, 2002).

Duncan, Michelle, 'Hydromancy: Of Sirens, Songs, and Soma' (unpublished paper, 2005).

Eco, Umberto, *Serendipities: Language and Lunacy* (New York/London: Phoenix, 1999).

Erlmann, Veit (ed.), *Hearing Cultures: Essays on Sound, Listening, and Modernity* (Oxford: Berg, 2004).

Eshun, Kodwo, *More Brilliant Than the Sun: Adventures in Sonic Fiction* (London: Quartet Books, 1998).

Feldman, Morton, *Give My Regards to Eighth Street* (Cambridge: Exact Change, 2000).

Finn, Geraldine, *Why Althusser Killed His Wife: Essays on Discourse and Violence* (Atlantic Highlands, NJ: Humanities Press, 1996).

Finn, Geraldine 'Giving Place – Making Space – For Truth – In Music' (unpublished paper).

Finn, Geraldine, 'To Speculate – On Music – and/as the Sound of *Différance*', *Dutch Journal for Music Theory* 7/3 (2002), pp. 189–95.

Fiumara, Gemma Corradi, *The Other Side of Language* (London/New York: Routledge. 1990).

Foucault, Michel, *The Order of Things: An Archeology of the Human Sciences*, trans. A. Shendan (New York: Pantheon Books, 1971).

Franssens, Joep (1997) 'Sound' (an interview with Johan Kolsteeg), *Key Notes* XXXI/1, pp. 20–23.

Gadamer, Hans Georg, *Truth and Method*, trans. G. Barden and J. Cumming (London: Sheed and Ward 1979).

Godwin, Joscelyn, *Harmonies of Heaven and Earth: The Spiritual Dimension of Music from Antiquity to the Avant-Garde* (London: Thames and Hudson, 1987).

Goehr, Lydia, *The Imaginary Museum of Musical Works* (Oxford: Oxford University Press, 1994).

Gouk, Penelope, 'Raising Spirits and Restoring Souls: Early Modern Medical Explanations for Music's Effects', in Erlmann, Veit (ed.), *Hearing Cultures: Essays on Sound, Listening, and Modernity* (Oxford: Berg, 2004).

Grey, De Sayles R., *John Coltrane and the 'Avant-Garde' Movement in Jazz History* (Pittsburgh, PA: University of Pittsburgh, 1986).

Griffiths, Paul, *Modern Music and After* (Oxford: Oxford University Press, 1995).

Harvey, Jonathan, *In Quest of Spirit: Thoughts on Music* (Berkeley, CA: University of California Press, 1999).

Haskins, Susan, *Mary Magdalen: Myth and Metaphor* (London: HarperCollins, 1993).

Heidegger, Martin, *Time and Being*, trans. J. Macquarrie (London: SCM Press, 1962).

Heidegger, Martin, *What is Called Thinking?*, trans. J. Glenn Gray (New York: Harper and Row, 1968).

Heidegger, Martin, 'The Origin of the Work of Art', in *Poetry, Language, Thought*, trans. A. Hofstadter (New York: Harper and Row, 1971).

Heidegger, Martin, 'Letter on Humanism' (1946), in *Pathmarks*, ed. William McNeill (Cambridge: Cambridge University Press, 1998), pp. 234–76.

Hesse, Hermann, *Siddharta* (London: Vision Press, 1960).

Hillier, Paul, *Arvo Pärt* (Oxford: Oxford University Press, 1997).

Hillis Miller, J., 'The Critic as a Host', in Harold Bloom (ed.), *Deconstruction and Criticism* (New York: Continuum, 1979).

Hirsbrunner, Theo, *Claude Debussy und seine Zeit* (Laaber: Laaber Verlag, 2003).

Horkheimer, Max and Adorno, Theodor, *Dialectic of Enlightenment*, trans. J. Cumming (London: Allen Lane, 1973).

Irigaray, Luce, *L'oubli de l'air chez Martin Heidegger* (Paris: Minuit, 1983).

James, Jamie, *The Music of the Spheres: Music, Science and the Natural Order of the Universe* (London: Abacus, 1995).

Jost, Ekkehard, *Free Jazz* (New York: Da Capo Press, 1994).

Kate, Laurens ten, *De lege plaats. Revoltes tegen het instrumentele leven in Bataille's atheologie* (Kampen: Kok Agora, 1994).

Kearney, Richard, *On Stories* (London/New York: Routledge, 2002).

Kockelmans, Joseph J., *On Heidegger and Language* (Evanston, IL: Northwestern University Press, 1972).

Koskoff, Ellen, 'Miriam Sings Her Song: The Self and the Other in Anthropological Discourse', in Ruth Solie (ed.), *Musicology and Difference: Gender and Sexuality in Music Scholarship* (Berkeley, CA: University of California Press, 1993), pp. 149–63.

Krausser, Helmut, *Melodien* (München/Leipzig: List Verlag, 1993).

Kristeva, Julia, *Revolution in Poetic Language*, trans. M. Waller (New York: Columbia University Press, 1984).

Leppert, Richard, *Essays on Music: Theodor W. Adorno* (Berkeley, CA: University of California Press, 2002).

Levin, David, *The Listening Self* (London/New York: Routledge, 1989).

Liebman, David, 'John Coltrane's *Meditations* Suite: A Study in Symmetry', in Henry Martin (ed.), *Annual Review of Jazz Studies 8* (Lanham, MD: Scarecrow Press, 1996).

Lyotard, Jean-François, *The Postmodern Condition*, trans. G. Bennington and B. Massumi (Minneapolis, MN: University of Minnesota Press, 1984a).

Lyotard, Jean-François, 'Several Silences', in *Driftworks* (New York: Semiotext(e), 1984b).

Lyotard, Jean-François, *The Differend: Phrases in Dispute*, trans. G. Van Den Abbeele (Minneapolis, MN: University of Minnesota Press, 1988).

Lyotard, Jean-François, *The Inhuman: Reflections on Time*, trans. G. Bennington and R. Bowlby (Cambridge: Polity Press, 1991).

Lyotard, Jean-François, *The Postmodern Explained: Correspondence 1982–1985*, trans. and eds J. Pefanis, M. Thomas, and D. Barry (Minneapolis, MN: University of Minnesota Press, 1993).

Mallarmé, Stéphane, *Oeuvres complètes* (Paris: Gallimard, 1945).

Martelaere, Patricia de, *Een verlangen naar ontroostbaarheid* (Amsterdam: Meulenhoff, 1994).

Merleau-Ponty, Maurice, *The Phenomenology of Perception*, trans. C. Smith (London/New York: Routledge and Kegan Paul, 1962).

Mulder, Etty, *De zang van vogelvrouwen. Psychoanalytische verkenningen in mythe en muziek* (Leiden: Plantage, 1994).

Nancy, Jean-Luc, *À l'écoute* (Paris: Galilée, 2002).

Nietzsche, Friedrich, *The Gay Science*, trans. W. Kaufmann (New York: Random House Inc, 1974).

Nietzsche, Friedrich, *Human, All Too Human*, trans. H. Zimmern, and P.V. Cohn (Mineola, NY: Dover Publications, 2006).

Proust, Marcel, *Swann's Way*, trans. C.K. Scott (New York: Heritage Press, 1954).

Rapaport, Herman, *Is There Truth in Art?* (Ithaca, NY: Cornell University Press, 1997).

Rouget, Gilbert, *Music and Trance: A Theory of the Relations between Music and Possession*, trans. B. Biebuyck (Chicago, IL: University of Chicago Press, 1985).

Saint-Exupéry, Antoine de, *Le Petit Prince* (Paris: Gallimard, 1999).

Sangild, Torben, 'Glitch – The Beauty of Malfunction', in Christopher J. Washburne and Maiken Derno (eds), *Bad Music: The Music We Love to Hate* (London/New York: Routledge, 2004), pp. 257–74.

Scheers, Rob van, 'De stilte en de naakte tonen', *Elsevier* (13 May 1989), pp. 117–23.

Schwarz, David, *Listening Subjects: Music, Psychology, Culture* (Durham, NC: Duke University Press, 1997).

Serres, Michel, *Statues* (Paris: Flammarion, 1993).

Sloterdijk, Peter, *Kopernikanische Mobilmachung und ptolemäische Abrüstung* (Frankfurt a/M: Suhrkamp Verlag, 1987).

Sloterdijk, Peter, *Weltfremdheit* (Frankfurt a/M: Suhrkamp Verlag, 1993).

Solomon, Robert C., *Spirituality for the Skeptic: The Thoughtful Love of Life* (Oxford: Oxford University Press, 2002).

Subotnik, Rose, *Deconstructive Variations: Music and Reason in Western Society* (Minneapolis, MN: University of Minnesota Press, 1996).

Taruskin, Richard, 'Music's Danger and the Case for Control', *New York Times*, Sunday, December 9, 2001, AR 1, 31.

Taylor, Mark C., *Erring: a Postmodern A/theology* (Chicago, IL: University of Chicago Press, 1984).

Taylor, Mark C., *Nots* (Chicago, IL: University of Chicago Press, 1993).

Taylor, Victor E., *Para/Inquiry: Postmodern Religion and Culture* (London/New York: Routledge, 1999).

Thomas, J.C., *Chasin' the Trane: The Music and Mystique of John Coltrane* (London: Elm Tree Books, 1975).

Ugrešić, Dubravka, *The Culture of Lies* (London: Phoenix, 1996).

Vattimo, Gianni, *After Christianity*, trans. L. d'Isanto (New York: Columbia University Press, 2002).

Vattimo, Gianni, *Belief*, trans. L. d'Isanto and D. Webb (Cambridge: Polity Press, 1999).

Vattimo, Gianni, *De transparante samenleving*, trans. H. Slager (Amsterdam: Boom, 1998).

Voorsluis, Bart, *Ongewone alledaagsheid. Spiritualiteit en het dagelijks leven.* (Zoetermeer: Meinema, 2003).

Watts, Alan W., *The Wisdom of Insecurity* (New York: Vintage Books, 1951).

Welsch, Wolfgang, *Unsere postmoderne Moderne* (Weinheim: VCH, Acta Humaniora, 1988).

Wilson, Peter Niklas, 'Sakrale Sehnsüchte, über den "unstillbaren ontologischen Durst" in der Musik der Gegenwart', in Helga de la Motte-Haber (ed.), *Musik und Religion* (Laaber: Laaber-Verlag, 1995), pp. 323–34.

Wittgenstein, Ludwig, *On Certainty*, trans. G.E.M. Anscombe and G.H. von Wright (Oxford: Blackwell, 1974).

Index